Acclaim for *Finding Common Ground*

"I think this book should be a prerequisite for managers of all kinds. It is impossible to operate in the 1990s in a profit or not-for-profit organization without understanding the legal climate we live in, and developing a strategy for coping with it. This book will provide a readable, interesting primer for that purpose."

—Peter B. Hawes, President and CEO, Design Professionals Insurance Co.

"Those involved in conflict will find this to be a lucid, comprehensive handbook for achieving a better way to resolve disputes."

—Malcolm K. Brachman, President, Northwest Oil Co.

"Everyone who deals with conflict—whether in business, in the home, in the community, in institutions, public or private—can gain a new perspective on the possibilities of mediation though this book. It ought to be required reading in law schools and business schools."

—Delos Putz, Professor, University of San Francisco Law School

"Barbara Phillips has given people unfamiliar with mediation and litigation a window into the world of lawyers, mediators, and courts. Her stories are engaging, and her emphasis on the transformative power of mediation should interest the professional as well as the neophyte."

—Linda R. Singer, mediator and author of *Settling Disputes*

"Phillips has written a most useful handbook to introduce mediation as the artful use of managed communication. Her work captures the staggering inefficiencies of today's litigation culture and makes the solid case for mediation as a better way. Throughout, she uses basic teaching techniques—colorful anecdotes, 'lessons learned,' easy-to-follow checklists, and others—to show how mediation can be a powerful tool to cut through contentious disputation and help build lasting consensus."

—Stephen B. Middlebrook, Senior Vice President and Executive Counsel, Aetna Life and Casualty Company

"Phillips explains why thoughtful people should be turning to mediation to resolve their disputes. Based on her extensive mediation practice, *Finding Common Ground* highlights the benefits of mediation, contrasting it to the destructive tendencies of litigation, which Phillips describes as a 'hovering specter.' This is an excellent explanation of the agreement model of mediation."

—Robert Coulson, President, American Arbitration Association

"*Finding Common Ground* fills a big gap in the field. It talks to potential users of mediation in a very concrete way about the process and how to approach using mediation and mediators. It is an exceptional book, and extremely useful. Mediators as well as clients will find this book very helpful. It suggests techniques which not all mediators will be familiar with, gives suggestions to clients that mediators will want to adopt for their clients, and looks at what mediators do in a very interesting way. Bravo! This book will become a classic."

—Zena Zumeta, former President of the Academy of Family Mediators

"I just finished reading *Finding Common Ground* and congratulate the author on a great job. My only disappointment was that I came to the last page when the pure enjoyment of reading the book came to an end. There are many books setting forth the nuts and bolts—that is, the 'what to do and how to do it' aspect of mediation. This book, however, involves a far deeper, yet eminently understandable treatment of the subject. In practical, human terms, Phillips has conveyed an understanding of what makes mediation work and why. The book is pure enjoyment to read and leaves the reader with an understanding of how to resolve anything ranging from run-of-the-mill to extremely complex disputes. The only persons for whom this is not a must read are those who have never been and never will be involved in a dispute."

—John H. Wilkinson, editor, *Donovan Leisure Newton & Irvine ADR Handbook*

'This book is a primer for professionals who are responsible for resolving disputes. It should be required reading for insurance claims executives, general counsel, and personnel directors."

—Richard Marrs, former Senior Vice President, Property/Casualty Claims, The Travelers Corporation

"Interesting and useful to the lawyer as well as the laymen. Eliminates the mystery of the mediation process."

—Edwin Kilburn, Vice President, ITT Corporation

"A great book for non-lawyer mediators. As a non-lawyer mediator, I found a wealth of insight in this little book to inform my practice. Barbara Phillips brings a deep wisdom and love of humanity to an incisive and penetrating analysis of mediation involving lawyers. Case after case in her clear, crisp style she shows how mediation humanizes and really works. I am grateful to her for writing this book."

—Margaret Huber, Training Coordinator, Center for Conflict Resolution, Justice Institute of British Columbia

"Ms. Phillips's book provides important insights and practical advice for advocates and their clients about the mediation process. Based on my mediation experience, she exposes the gamesmanship that frequently confounds efforts to settle litigation and shows how mediation can provide successful resolution."

—Louise A. LaMothe, former Chair, Section of Litigation, American Bar Association

"I see [*Finding Common Ground*] as an extremely valuable source and text for mediation and alternative dispute resolution training."

—Harry C. Geissler, Florida mediator

"In *Finding Common Ground*, Barbara Phillips, one of mediation's true pioneers, has written a book that assists readers to understand the science and the art of mediation and the importance of mediation in our social evolution."

—James Melamed, Chair, Oregon Dispute Resolution Commission, founding President and Executive Director of the Oregon Mediation Assoc., and professor of negotiation and mediation, University of Oregon School of Law.

"*Finding Common Ground* is not only an excellent explanation of the mediation process, it is something much more. It is an articulate statement of how mediation works—how it affects us as lawyers and our clients. It gives you a great feel for the subtleties and importance of the process. There's been much written in the field of mediation recently, but Phillips's book is new and different. It explains mediation from inside out, not only the process, but more importantly, the heart and feel of this new and important means of resolving our disputes. I highly recommend it."

—J. Gary Gwilliam, former President, California Trial Lawyers Assoc.

"If you want to know why mediation is becoming so popular and wish to use it (or even just become more familiar with the subject, or improve your skills as a mediator), read this excellent book. It describes the various mediation processes that are available and why they may be preferable to litigation in resolving your disputes. Explanations are interspersed not only with careful instructions on the procedures, but also with accounts of actual mediations with which the author, as an experienced practitioner, is familiar."

—Robert D. Raven, Chair, American Bar Assoc., Dispute Resolution Section

"In *Finding Common Ground*, Barbara Phillips provides an articulate, accessible overview of the mediation process. Whether the dispute belongs in small claims court or on the world stage, Ms. Phillips makes a powerful argument for choosing mediation over more adversarial processes. By breaking down the mediation process into its component parts, Ms. Phillips illuminates why mediation can be so successful and why mediation can successfully counter 'lit-think.' This book will be a valuable resource for consumers of mediation, for lawyers involved in mediation, and for experienced mediators."

— Melanie C. Greenberg, Deputy Director, Stanford Center on Conflict and Negotiation, Stanford University

"This book is filled with practical advice that springs from the experience of the author. It is a must for those interested in mediation. Anyone needing to know more about mediation will want to get this book."

—James J. Brosnahan, Morrison & Foerster, San Francisco, Calif.

Finding Common Ground

A Field Guide to Mediation

Barbara Ashley Phillips

Hells Canyon Publishing
Austin, Texas
Halfway, Oregon

Hells Canyon Publishing, Inc.
P.O. Box 646, Halfway, Oregon, 97834

Published by Hells Canyon Publishing, Inc., Halfway, Ore.
First printing, 1994

Publisher's Cataloging in Publication Data

Phillips, Barbara Ashley
Finding Common Ground : a field guide to mediation / by Barbara Ashley Phillips. — 1st ed. — Halfway, Ore. : Hells Canyon Pub., c1994.
p. cm.
Includes bibliographic references and index.
ISBN 0-9633919-7-6
1. Mediation. 2. Dispute resolution (Law).
I. Title.
347.09 94-75151

Printed in the United States of America
First Edition

Cover design by Lightbourne Images

Versions of Chapters 7, *Evaluating Mediation;* 9, *Preparing for Mediation*; and Appendix 4, *Family Mediation,* have appeared in The Alternative Dispute Resolution Practice Guide, Roth, Wulff and Cooper, editors, Lawyers Co-operative Publishing Co., 1993.

The material in Appendices 3, 4 and 5 is used with the permission of Kenneth C. Cloke, with whom the author collaborated.

This book is dedicated to my sons,
John and Matthew Phillips, whose
generation may well make collaborative
processes its signature.

Contents

Foreword

No one enmeshed in the civil justice system is satisfied that litigation is a desirable means of resolving disputes. Litigation is terribly expensive, slow, cumbersome and uncertain in its outcome. Nevertheless, business, labor and ordinary citizens who have suffered injuries or other grievances still crowd the dockets of courts all over the United States. Many of them continue to believe that lawsuits are as inevitable as death and taxes. As Barbara Phillips explains in *Finding Common Ground*, settlement of disputes through mediation, rather than litigation, can resolve civil controversies of many kinds with far better results, far earlier, and far cheaper than litigation.

In easy prose, Ms. Phillips explains how we got ourselves into this fix and how, in many instances, we can get ourselves back out again. She takes her readers step-by-step through a successful mediation process to demonstrate how mediation can work and what it can do for the disputants when assisted by a skilled neutral mediator. She should know because she has successfully mediated a wide variety of difficult controversies.

I commend *Finding Common Ground* to lawyers and judges as well as to companies and individuals who find themselves embroiled in seemingly intractable controversies and who want to find a better way to resolve their differences than saying to their adversaries: "I'll see you in court."

Shirley M. Hufstedler
first U.S. Secretary of Education
(Carter Administration)
February, 1994

Acknowledgments

Acknowledgments provide an opportunity to reflect on gifts of time and attention that are beyond price. Among those whose vision and inspiration have helped me through various stages of this process are Marg Huber, Delos Putz, Toni Rembe, Ted Phillips, Ted Goodwin, Allan Littman, Peter Hawes, Susan Hammer, John L. Miller, Bill Oler, Dick Marrs, Janis Sue Porter, Sidney Lezak, Peter Lovenheim, Bill Lincoln, Joel Edelman, Ken Cloke, Dave Jones, Mal Brachman, Louise LaMothe, Linda Singer, Jim Brosnahan, Deborah Kolb, Bob Raven, Gary Gwilliam, Shirley Hufstedler, Carla Hills, Elaine Hallmark, Melanie Greenberg, Ellen Beilock, Jim Melamed and many others who have read and commented on various drafts. This book could not have been completed without the assistance of Holly Sanders of Halfway, Oregon.

The alumni of AIS, American Intermediation Service, our once-upon-a-time flagship of what we thought the best in mediation might be, are also contributors to the thinking and experience reflected here. Among them are Arlen Gregorio, Susan Haldeman, David Jenkins, Judith Roberts and Tony Piazza, as well as Jude Bedell, Benbow Bullock, Elsie Dawson, Tom Tabakin, Suzanne Perry Page, Chris Amerio, Marty Blum, Matt and John Phillips, Lynne Howe and many others. The lawyers and clients I have mediated with have taught me many times over about the permutations and requirements for doing quality mediation. My teachers, Edith Stauffer, Buck Ghosthorse and Galen Drapeau have fostered a growing understanding of what it means to live a fully evolved life. And I thank my friends, especially Patricia Sowers, David Light, Buffy Black, Mary Gaynor and Sandra Aragon, for their vision of what my life might become, and their belief in my ability to produce this book to communicate my passion.

Introduction

Mediation does not reveal itself readily: sessions are private and highly confidential. As gatekeepers of the process, mediators are reluctant to speak without heavily disguising the event, in order to preserve confidentiality.

This is a personal book, based on my own experience as a mediator and a concerned professional for more than 13 years and as a litigator and trial lawyer for 20 years before that. It is also based on my experience as a consumer of both legal and mediation services.

This is a book about mediation of matters affecting businesses and organizations. Most are already in litigation. An exception is Chapter 13, *Charting Public and Private Policy,* which is included to illustrate the power of mediation and facilitation on the affairs of our community, state and nation. Appendices 4 and 5 are included because family conflict has much to teach about mediation.

This book showcases the significant benefits of mediating nearly any conflict at any stage. Examples are drawn from contract disputes, construction projects, class actions, sexual harassment suits, resource and land issues, intellectual property disputes, property damage cases, employment disputes, personal injury suits, intra-organizational problems, community and interpersonal conflicts and parental communication problems.

Mediation's success in no way detracts from the importance of our American legal system. The need for a formal civil justice system that can command the attendance of parties and witnesses and make enforceable judgments is not disputed. What is at issue is the suitability and appropriateness of adversarial processes to the vast majority of lawsuits and potential lawsuits which ultimately will be resolved through negotiation. Indeed, it is the hovering specter of full-blown litigation that makes the effective use of mediation so compelling.

I have written this book for leaders who need their own window on the mediation process, for business and professional users of mediation, for established mediators and aspiring mediators, for lawyers, judges and claims professionals, for human resources professionals and anyone else who wants a thorough understanding of a simple and effective approach to mediation. Most case examples involve lawyers, as lawyers are the gate-keepers of the legal system, from which most of the cases here have come. That does not mean that they are about a heavily lawyered type of mediation. Quite the contrary.

The more "lawyered" a process or proceeding, the more time-consuming and cumbersome it is. Litigation and arbitration have felt the increasing weight of this reality in the past two to three decades, as the information revolution has reached the legal profession. Mediation is still fresh, spontaneous and alive because so many mediators are not lawyers or are lawyers who have made it a point to put aside much of their legalistic approach to things.

Mediation is no monolith. We are only beginning to define what it is that makes for good in mediation. Some individuals become mediators with little or no mediation training, having perhaps read an article or attended a program on mediation. They assess themselves reasonably personable and persuasive, with some understanding of the compulsory model of judicial settlement-conferencing. What they often offer is an adversarial mediation, marked by controlling behavior and advice-giving.

The agreement model of mediation is very different and is being defined more and more clearly through studies reported recently by the National Institute for Dispute Resolution (NIDR). In the hands of a skilled mediator, it draws people out, helps lower defenses, banishes unrealistic optimism and pessimism and lowers frustration. People are restored to their own good judgment and regain a sense of balance and proportion.

This book is about the agreement model of mediation, here called *traditional* mediation. It is about lawyers, mediators and clients, whether business or personal. I want to speak to clients, for I have been one. I also want lawyers to see things from the client's perspective, a view too easy to ignore.

Transaction costs in handling disputes in American society are truly staggering and are growing daily. There is an old Chinese proverb that says, unless we change our direction, we are likely to end up where we are headed. The increasingly confrontational way we are headed is contrary to our best interests. Consider the words of Edgar Mitchell, Astronaut, viewing earth from the moon:

> It was a beautiful, harmonious, peaceful-looking planet, blue with white clouds, and one that gave you a deep sense . . . of home, of being, of identity. It is what I prefer to call instant global consciousness.

The old way is also, arguably, contrary to our true nature. In the past generation, archaeological discoveries of Dr. Marija Gimbutas and others have revealed the existence of a golden age of peace covering much of Europe, long before the rise of Indo-Europeans. This period lasted for more than twenty thousand years and ended about thirty five hundred years B.C., except in Crete and other Aegean and Mediterranean regions where it continued until 1500 B.C. Eventually, the patriarchal herding societies of Northern Europe attacked and overcame these peaceful, agrarian cultures south of them. (Gimbutas, *The Language of the Goddess,* Harper and Row, 1989, Introduction)

The peacefulness of peoples in these times is inferred by scholars from the absence of celebration of battles and warriors in the work of their artists. It is only a step to the conclusion that the nature of humankind is not necessarily to be violent and war-like, despite evidence to the contrary from recorded history to the present time.

The agreement model of mediation reveals the threads which connect us one to another, so that we can keep those which are salutary and sever those which restrict. What is within our own power to affect or change becomes clear. We became free again to act in our own best interests.

Barbara Ashley Phillips
Halfway, Oregon
April 29, 1994

All of the mediations and convening events described in this book are true, although all names and locations have been changed. The sex of the mediator has been changed, as needed, for balance. At times, I have also combined features of several cases to further protect confidentiality and the anonymity of parties.

PART 1

Litigation and Beyond

A story is told of a town with one lawyer. He starved out and became a carpenter. Then another lawyer moved to town. Soon they both had more law business than they could handle.

1.
THE BIG SECRET

We dance round in a ring and suppose,
But the Secret sits in the middle
and knows. — Robert Frost

It was a warm summer day in Seattle. The lawyers were polite. It was obvious there was only one person at the table who believed there was any hope the matter could settle. Lawyers for the plaintiff class were there out of courtesy to the mediator who had invited them to spend a day seeing what progress could be made. Defense counsel was going through the motions for his client, who initiated this mediation.

The dispute had been the subject of three lawsuits lasting more than four years. There had never been any negotiations. Each side was committed to winning . . . but it had been a long time since anyone asked what "winning" meant.

In the next eight hours, something important happened. The mediator listened, asked questions, caucused with each side time and again. She showed the parties they needed to know more about what the actual damages might turn out to be, if the plaintiffs prevailed. They discovered this information could be developed fairly readily. It was agreed to recess and meet again in two weeks. There was cautious optimism, as the parties saw that they could at least agree on what was needed, who would get it and when to reconvene. By the end of the second day of mediation, the rough outlines of a settlement had been reached. The details were polished off in a third day, six weeks after the initial session. Hundreds of workers affected by this lawsuit got the benefits of the settlement and for everyone, the ordeal was over.

How long would this case have continued to be litigated without mediation? We can only say that this four-year-old dispute resolved in mediation, as do most matters mediated. We know the high success rate in mediation is independent of the dispute's maturity. Impending wrongful termination disputes resolve in mediation before the termination. Intra-family disputes resolve in mediation before the family relationship has died. Contract disputes between businesses resolve in mediation allowing business relationships to be productively resumed.

The secret is that whatever the dispute, it's very likely to settle. Ninety percent of disputes never reach the courts. Nearly ninety-five percent of those that do, resolve without ever going to trial. This suggests that Americans are passionately determined to resolve their own disputes — despite the biggest and most costly lawsuit industry in the world.

There is some evidence that the law business is facing a decline in growth rate. In the early 1990s, for the first time in decades law firms are hurting. Reductions in large law firm ranks approach thirty percent in many cases. The reasons for this are complex, but the inexorable move of disputants toward mediation and other litigation alternatives is a factor.[1]

What Is Litigation?

Litigation is not trial. It is preparing for the trial that, ninety-five percent of the time, won't happen. Litigation is taking "discovery," formal inquiry into the matter by written questions, recorded interrogation and requests for production of documents. Interrogatories — questions posed in writing — are often easy to evade. Litigation involves devising answers that duck the questions.

Litigation is taking depositions — oral testimony under oath of truthfulness — to get information or to "pin down" the witness to make it hard to say something different at the trial that will almost never take place. Deposition transcripts are prepared by long-suffering court reporters and transcribers. To make these long and boring depositions useful, lawyers or paralegals then spend more hours summarizing them.

Parties in litigation often are required to produce all manner of business records, files and other papers by the box and even in carload lots. These are called document productions. They tell both more and less than they should, but tell almost nothing about how the matter might properly be resolved.

In litigation, lawyers appear in court to answer questions that make it easier for the court to manage its calendar;[2] they make or defend motions which sometimes complicate, rather than simplify, the situation; and they seek emergency orders (rarely granted) and to explain lapses and delays. New York lawyer and litigator, John H. Wilkinson, passes along the following story:

> Explaining how the law works to a group of high school students, a prominent bar member recently stated, "You spend years and years in pretrial motion practice. I smother the other side with papers and they smother me with papers until we wear each other out and the judge knocks my head against his head and we settle. It takes about three or four years."[3]

Like war, as Winston Churchill said, litigation is "mainly a catalogue of blunders."

One Los Angeles lawyer observed, "I have sinned. I cannot think of a case I have tried without stacks of depositions and boxes of organized and indexed but unnecessary documents. But that's the way I was trained and that's what the clients seem to want." You, as client, hold the reins. Will you use them?

Courts recognize the wastefulness of litigation activity. Judges believe getting to trial in less than five years will help force people to resolve their differences. So they adopt fast track programs that require a lot of litigation activity right away, when no one knows if it will ever be necessary. This is expensive.

Recognizing that most cases settle, courts have begun to adopt mandatory mediation rules, which force people to sit down together and talk in the presence of a disinterested third party, usually a lawyer and sometimes a mediator. This can undercut the voluntariness that makes mediation so effective.[4]

What Is Mediation?

Mediation can rise to the level of diplomacy, but unlike litigation, it cannot fall to the level of a street brawl. It is a negotiation moderated by a neutral party to resolve conflict in ways that meet the parties' interests.[5] The principals may participate fully.

In commercial mediation, there is usually a joint session that may run from one-half hour to several hours or even a full day. Here, the parties orally inform the mediator about the situation. This is followed by caucuses — private meetings between the mediator and each side — commonly used in business mediation. In these private meetings or caucuses, three things happen. First, a party can give the mediator confidential information it did not want to disclose in the joint session.[6] Second, the mediator will disclose what he sees as that side's hurdles, weaknesses, problems. Finally, these private caucuses allow creativity and a certain anonymity as to the source of ideas about ways of resolving the matter. Trust, often absent at the beginning, builds gradually as little agreements are reached and people notice that their concerns are being addressed. The mediator works with both sides, and sometimes with the experts and counsel, often keeping people civil to each other just by being there.

The mediator may be briefed in advance of the mediation. (See Chapter 9, *Preparing to Mediate*.) He convenes the mediation, outlining the procedure and inviting agreement on certain ground rules. After the confidentiality agreement is signed, he listens to the presentations and reframes them in summary form, highlighting what's important by the attention given to certain points. In caucuses, participants share with the mediator what they won't share with the other side. The mediator also helps each side to see the other's point of view and helps develop options for resolution, as the parties come to a new perspective on their dispute.

Who's In Control?

In litigation, lawyers think they are in control. Judges think they are in control. Clients sometimes think they are in control. In fact, no one is in control, nor is the litigation under control. Once begun, litigation has a life of its own. It feeds on clients, lawyers and judges, all of whom become paler, but somehow usually keep walking and talking. Many lawyers feel trapped by the profession they once loved.

Mediation is a different story. Generally in civil lawsuit mediation, the lawyer makes the presentation and response. The lawyer advises the client on the reasonableness of settlement options, for it is the client's decision. The mediator is in charge of the process. The clients or principals are in charge of all decisions. They need stay only so long as it is productive.

Litigation Isn't Working For Us Anymore

Our court system was developed in England for a very different society and time to deal with problems very different from ours. In the U.S. it suffers from overdevelopment and has grown both form-driven and rule-driven, as courts struggle to keep up with the tidal wave of litigation.[7]

The system turns some lawyers into legal gladiators ". . . poised to grab a large retainer and begin billing hours for all that the war will require. Endless discovery and the full panoply of motions will be necessary. Nothing is to be conceded. Only the complete surrender of the enemy or the mandate of the court of last resort can end this dispute."[8] Fifth Circuit Judge Thomas Reavley describes this kind of lawyer as ". . . a dinosaur of our times and a threat to every unfortunate client who enters his office."[9] Few lawyers fit this description today, though the dreadnaught mentality persists in many plush temples of the law.

We have a contingent fee system in which counsel often advance costs to guarantee access to the legal system for many who could not otherwise have it. But with the increasing complexity of discovery and pre-trial practices, this comes close to

A Third Party Decides		The Parties Decide	
Arbitration	informal, limited appeal	**Negotiation**	direct discussions; agreements non-appealable
Court trial	court decides law and facts; appealable	**Mediation**	facilitated discussions; agreements non-appealable
Jury Trial	jury decides facts; court decides law; appealable		

Hybrid
Advisory Mediation

Neutral advises parties of:
probable outcome of litigation
or
opinion on the merits.
Agreements are not appealable

Fig. 1 Dispute Resolution Models

requiring a banker rather than a lawyer. It is no accident that we have seen shares in lawsuits sold in recent years. It is no better for defendants who may end up spending far more on legal fees and expenses than the case itself is worth.

No small part of the burgeoning cost of litigation is due to the intricacy of claims and defenses and the lack of deterrents within the system to prevent delay for delay's sake.[10] There are also ethical constraints which serve to hinder and delay the prosecution of cases: a lawyer's primary professional risk is to fail to assert a claim or defense. Thus cases are tried on all possible theories in a climate where theories are proliferating, causing trials and arbitrations to take vastly more time and money than is necessary. In this way the system rewards breadth rather than clarity of focus.

Few people know that when they retain counsel, it is likely to be two to five years before they see any results.[11] For the plaintiffs in serious injury cases, such delay can mean lives of quiet desperation as they try to cope with their condition without the needed financial resources.

When you spend years litigating only to eventually settle the case by negotiation, you've done the equivalent of traveling from Chicago to New York by way of Los Angeles. True, you will reach your destination. But it is a habit worth breaking.

Lit-think escalates disputes. "Lit-think" is our preoccupation with litigation. When litigation is even just outside "the picture," people often stop behaving constructively. Business people stop trying to work things out and rush to the barricades, each side believing the other side is just trying to set them up (since they are trying to set up the other side). Frequently, the motives we ascribe to others are our own motives, safely hidden from our conscious minds.

This destructive way of thinking about disputes — that we are engaged in war — in fact jeopardizes our interests. War requires that in order for us to win, the other side must lose. That is a formidable hurdle to achieving success in resolving the difficulties that brought us to seek counsel in the first place.

Justice and the justice system are not the same. It is more productive to think of litigation as a tool, one of several ways of securing results. The fact that it is commonplace has raised our threshold of outrage. We need to be re-sensitized. When an obstetrician's malpractice insurance runs more than $70,000 per year, when ice skating rinks and playgrounds are closing because of inability to secure insurance at all, isn't it time we noticed?[12]

As Robert Ornstein and Paul Ehrlich point out in *New World, New Mind*, our old minds handle gradual change quite poorly.

Once we are conditioned to a situation, whether it be nuclear explosions or acid rain or the decay of our infrastructure, it ceases to be important. It is, as these authors point out, another example of the boiled frog syndrome. A frog sitting in a pan of water which is gradually heated will not recognize the risk and will die rather than jump out, even though a frog dropped into hot water will bound away instantly. We have much to learn from frogs about what it takes to survive in this world of ours.

How Does Litigation Serve?

Legislation is usually described as the way for the law to evolve. In the U.S., litigation serves this purpose also, in part because our legislative process leaves a lot more to the discretion of courts than it does in the English system.[13] Many liabilities have evolved through litigation — the liability of doctors, hospitals, manufacturers, mechanics, lawyers. It has been the courts that established so many new responsibilities: skating rink owners for skaters, doctors and drug manufacturers for deformed babies. And many of the rights declared through legislation — such as the right to an environment free of discrimination based on age, race, sex, national origin, handicap — are given life by the courts. The increasing complexity of technical defenses may result in court decisions that encourage patterns of resistance rather than patterns of compliance — all in ways very costly to litigants.

Can Mediation Help The Law Evolve?

Probably not. The law has evolved through decision after decision in case after case. Would people negotiating in good faith change rules of liability and the extent of damages without judicial precedent? It is unlikely.[14] But even today, precedent is established by only a small percentage of cases.

What mediation can do, so long as it is voluntary, is to meet the needs of individuals and organizations to find out whether a satisfactory outcome is available through negotiation. Contrary to widespread belief, it can do so at almost any stage of the matter.

For cases that will never be tried, this eliminates most of the transaction costs and delay. The cases that must be tried will be easier to identify and may be handled, perhaps more effectively, by courts that will at last have the time to deal with them.

Notes to Chapter 1

1. Steven Brill, "Headnotes: The New Leverage," The American Lawyer, July/August 1993, pp. 65, 66.

2. In the federal courts in 1989 the case load per judge was 489 filed cases per judge, 407 of which were civil filings. Report of the Director, Administrative Office of the U.S. Courts, Twelve Month Period Ended June 30, 1989 - Appendix 1, Detailed Statistical Tables 36 (1989) Tables 36 (1989), note 14 at p. 134. Little wonder that judges have become fanatical about calendar management.

   Some of this anxiety about the litigation explosion may be outdated, however. The California Judicial Council, for example, reports little change in the number of civil suits per capita filed in that state, since 1960. *Justice in the Balance, Report of the Commission on the Future of the California Courts,* California Judicial Council, February, 1994. The Report states: "With 6,000 civil filings per 100,000 residents, [California is] well below the national median."

3. From the comprehensive book, *Donovan Leisure Newton & Irvine ADR Practice Book,* John H. Wilkinson, ed., John Wiley & Sons, 1990, Preface.

4. One of the big debates in the mediation field is over voluntariness. Proponents of compulsory mediation argue that since settlement percentages in mandatory programs are similar to those in voluntary programs, it is irrelevant that people were forced into mediating. There is some evidence that satisfaction in child custody mediations is high, whether voluntary or mandatory. *Mediation, Law, Policy and Practice,* Rogers and McEwen, Lawyers Co-operative Pub. Co., 1989, Sec. 5.2, p. 47.

   The Society for Professionals in Dispute Resolution (SPIDR) issued a report on January 5, 1991 concluding that mandating participation in non-binding processes was appropriate, but needed to follow certain guidelines, among them that "coercion to settle in the form of reports to the trier of fact and of financial disincentives. . ." should not be used and that party and counsel participation, at the parties' option, be available. SPIDR *Mandated Participation and Settlement Coercion: Dispute Resolution as it Relates to the Courts,* Report 1 of the Committee on Law and Public Policy, 1990.

Some opponents of compulsory mediation stress lack of mediator training in regard to abusive relationships and the lack of protection for women in mandatory programs for child custody matters. See the seminal article by Trina Grillo, *The Mediation Alternative: Process Dangers for Women,* Yale Law Journal, 100:1545 (1991). Professor Grillo describes the world of California mandatory custody mediation in which mediators make recommendations to judges (thereby giving them significant coercive power). She identifies an *equal blame* hypothesis as guiding mediator interventions, thereby turning an empowering process into one in which the oppressed spouses are "forced to acquiesce in their own oppression." (p. 1610) Both of these are inconsistent with the values of the agreement model of mediation. Professor Joshua D. Rosenberg notes that in the subject program, the parties have little or no choice of mediators, the mediators have little time to spend on each case and lawyers usually are excluded. "In Defense of Mediation," 1991, 33 *Arizona Law Review* 467.

It is no surprise, then, that mandatory mediation is opposed on the grounds that it corrupts the process. I agree that making mediation mandatory exerts subtle and not-so-subtle pressures on the parties and the mediator. See endnote 12, below, for references to another line of attack on mediation.

However, in farmer-creditor mediations, the very viability of the programs seems to depend upon making it mandatory on the lender, once the farmer requests it. See also Linda Singer, *Settling Disputes,* "Mediating Between Farmers and Lenders," Westview Press, 1990, pp. 95-98, pointing out that unless lenders are compelled to mediate on the farmer's request, the process is little used. The key point here may be that institutional parties, such as lenders and government agencies, may need some compulsion to act in their own longer-term interests. It is all too easy for bureaucrats and administrators to get stuck in a short-term perspective.

5. Lon Fuller, one of the visionaries in the field of mediation, describes it this way: "It is obvious that [negotiation] . . . can often be greatly

facilitated through the services of a skillful mediator. His assistance can speed the negotiations, reduce the likelihood of miscalculation, and generally help the parties to reach a sounder agreement, an adjustment of their divergent valuations that will produce something like an optimum yield of the gains of reciprocity. These things the mediator can accomplish by holding separate confidential meetings with the parties, where each party gives the mediator a relatively full and candid account of the internal posture of his own interests. Armed with this information, but without making a premature disclosure of its details, the mediator can then help to shape the negotiations in such a way that they will proceed most directly to their goal, with a minimum of waste and friction . . ." Lon Fuller, "Mediation—Its Forms and Functions," 44 *So. California Law Review,* 1971, pp. 305, 307-309, 318, 324, 327-330.

6. There are several concerns that need to be addressed by agreements of confidentiality. They are:

   1. Admissibility in a later proceeding in the same case;
   2. Discoverability in a later proceeding in the same case;
   3. Required disclosure and admissibility through subpoena or depositions in other cases;
   4. Revelation to third parties. Note, "Protecting Confidentiality in Mediation," 98 *Harvard Law Review,* 1984, p. 441.

   Usually, these are addressed by contract—an agreement made before or at the commencement of mediation which binds the parties. Also there are rules of evidence (such as Rule 408 of the Federal Rules of Civil procedure, which is mirrored in the rules of many states), court-created privileges and special statutes. See *Confidentiality in Mediation: A Practitioner 's Guide,* American Bar Association, 1985, compiled by Lawrence Freedman, Christopher Haile and Howard Bookstaff. Many states have strengthened the protection for mediation, since this guide was published. While others cannot usually be bound by contracts to which they are not party, there is moral suasion arising from the need to protect the integrity of the mediation process which can effectively prevent outsiders from violating the spirit of the confidentiality to which the parties have committed.

   For the argument that iron-clad protection is not as necessary as the technically-minded might believe, see Eric Green, "A Heretical

View of the Mediation Privilege," 2 *Ohio State Journal of Dispute Resolution,* 1986, p. 1 .

7. Much of the time spent by the courts is spent on criminal cases. In 1988, the San Diego Superior Court suspended all civil trials indefinitely in order to work down the criminal docket backlog. Santa Clara County, also in California, suspended civil trials for 2 months to do a criminal docket purge. These courts are now fairly current on civil cases but at the heavy expense imposed by Fast Track. (See Chapter 3, n. 5.) In some courts, as little as 15% of trial time is available for civil trials. Little wonder that civil trials are so rare. See also 46 *Arbitration Journal* 3, Sept. 1991.

8. Hon. Thomas M. Reavley, Circuit Judge, U.S. Court of Appeals for the Fifth Circuit, "Consider Our Consumers," 14 *Pepperdine Law Review,* 1987, pp. 787, 788. Not a few voices are raised to challenge the ethics of lawyers who offer only litigation to resolve clients' problems. See Burkhardt and Conover, II, "The Ethical Duty to Consider Alternatives to Litigation," *The Colorado Lawyer,* February, 1990, pp. 249-251.

9. See note 8.

10. Court delay-reduction (Fast Track) programs may also be contributors to the burgeoning cost of litigation. See Chapter 3, note 5.

11. See Alschuler, "Mediation With a Mugger: The Shortage of Adjudicative Services and the Need for a Two Tier Trial System in Civil Cases," 99 *Harvard Law Review,* 1986, pp. 1808, 1822, and T. Church, Jr., A. Carlson, J. Lee & T. Tan, *Justice Delayed: The Pace of Litigation in Urban Trial Courts,* 1978 [describing findings of a national research project on inefficiency in the courts].

12. The damage to our quality of life from litigation filed without regard to its societal consequences is incalculable. A homeowner in an adult community with a minimum residence age of 45 becomes pregnant. She sues and breaks the covenant limiting residents to adults. All over California, adult communities raise their minimum age to 55, decreasing the age diversity of their groups and denying others like herself access at all. One may ask, was this trip necessary?

    Or take another situation: does the family whose child was

injured at a playground think about the possibility that their suit and others like it will lead to closure of this and other playgrounds (not necessarily through verdicts but because of insurance premiums, and an unwillingness to operate without that insurance)? Would they like to have had the opportunity to spread the risk of their actual loss (limited damages) without such consequences, through a quality negotiation process?

Peter Huber estimates that damages for accidents and personal injury cost individuals, businesses, municipalities and other government agencies more than $80 billion a year, noting the absence of swimming pools, slides and certain prescription drugs (legal to make, though no one will make them, he says, because of the risk of litigation). He gives as examples the great cost increases in other products, for example, that liability insurance costs 95% of the cost of childhood vaccines and 30% of the price of a stepladder, (although the basis for these estimates has been seriously questioned). *Liability,* Peter W. Huber, Basic Books, Inc., New York, 1988, pp. 3, 4.

13. Robert Summers and Patrick Atiyah, in an engaging book, *Form and Substance in Anglo-American Law,* (Clarendon Press, Oxford), 1987, examine the underpinnings of English and American decision-making and legal institutions. It is comforting to see how much of the burden of transforming the law that has fallen to the American courts is structural, rather than merely temperamental. Those who would reduce the law-making function of American courts may find guidance here.

14. Robert P. Burns writes on the appropriateness of mediation, describing the lively debate on whether there is a duty to have cases tried. See "The Appropriateness of Mediation: A Case Study and Reflection on Fuller and Fiss," 4 *Journal on Dispute Resolution p.* 129 and following. (1988). See also, Fiss, "Against Settlement," 93 *Yale Law Journal* pp. 1073-90 (1984); Menkel-Meadow, "For and Against Settlement: Uses and Abuses of the Mandatory Settlement Conference," 33 *UCLA Law Review,* pp. 485-514 (1985); Resnik, "Due Process: A Public Dimension," 39 *University of Florida Law Review,* Spr., 1987.

2.
MEDIATION IN ACTION

Be assured that if you knew all,
you would pardon all. — Thomas à Kempis

Mediation of matters already in litigation is the inheritor of the encrusted roles, attitudes and positions the adversarial process engenders. So long as the lit-think facade remains intact, the minimal trust essential to progress remains elusive. Interpersonal mediations share the hurdle of distrust, and benefit from similar techniques to overcome it. The following two stories are examples of the transformative power of mediation.

A Case Of Humility

Charlie Jacobson was in the prime of his career as a litigator — a partner in a large firm in a medium-sized city in the Midwest. He wasn't the first to defend this case: it had been pending for 13 years in federal court. But he had devoted enough of his life to it that he devoutly wished it would be over. Nevertheless, good soldier that he was, he continued the meticulous defense work that was his hallmark, fighting every issue he could find with excellent research and long argument, and with the approval, at least by default, of his corporate client.

It was a court-certified class-action based on racial and ethnic discrimination, brought by a group of sanitation workers against a waste disposal company. On the plaintiffs' side was a blind lawyer whose listening skills were to test the mediator. The case was being handled on a contingent fee basis, meaning the plaintiffs' lawyers would be paid only if and when they won. They were passionate in their advocacy and in their sense of outrage at what had happened to their clients and what seemed to be continuing to happen. Excellent lawyers, they were appalled that there had never been settlement talks in the case. Yet like Charlie, they were fully convinced such talks would do no good.

A new management team from the company brought in a mediator, who persuaded the plaintiffs' counsel to participate in mediated negotiations. Charlie seemed hostile to the mediation. It was suggested that this was because settling was against his economic interests (he was being paid hourly), and that it was part of his way of life to punish the uppity plaintiffs for the impertinence of bringing the suit in the first place. If they could only know how tired he was of this case.

The plaintiffs were asking more than $15 million. The employer's negotiators seemed to think $1 million would be more than enough. The mediation took only three days — two days of negotiation spaced two weeks apart and a final day a few weeks later to complete the details of a complex settlement agreement that required the approval of the union and the court.

After the initial joint session, the mediator focused tightly in the private caucuses on the specifics of the damage claims. Each party became involved in looking at possible ranges of recovery and some probabilities relating to them. During the first day, the mediator drew from the parties the best case and worst case scenarios, and encouraged the parties to devise non-economic elements to be included in any settlement package.

As progress became apparent, the mood shifted from hopelessness and bare civility to cautious optimism. The managers felt hurt that the plaintiffs had not acknowledged the tremendous effort made to correct workforce inequities and discrimination, such as the old boy network, favoritism and frequent racial and ethnic slurs. They therefore distrusted the plaintiffs' sincerity. On the other side, the plaintiffs' counsel continued to chafe at the apparent callousness of the defendant, as experienced through Charlie's defense.

At one point, the mediator had a brief moment with Charlie

alone. Charlie had been going through the motions in the mediation, but it was plain his heart wasn't in it. Sensing an opportunity, the mediator asked, "Do you have a family?" It had been a long day. Both were tired and hungry. Before long, Charlie spoke softly of his little girl and how much he missed seeing her grow up. Gone was the brittle facade of the litigation lawyer. They talked about the difficulties of combining career with family life. The moment passed, as others returned. Yet Charlie was changed. He was gentler in demeanor and much more creative in helping his client figure out how to structure a settlement that would work.

At another point a little later, the plaintiffs were ready to walk out. Had the plaintiffs' blind lawyer detected more commitment to settlement in the mediator than in himself? When the mediation begins, the mediator is empowered by the parties' mutual commitment to resolving, if they can reach a satisfactory resolution. It is easy for mediators to forget the limits of that mandate in the heat of mediation. Reminding himself that it was the parties' case, not his, the mediator backed off. "If you decide you don't want to settle this case, that's okay," he told the plaintiffs' caucus. It is hard to come this close to resolving and walk out, particularly after 13 years of litigation. After a long discussion among themselves, plaintiffs' counsel decided to see it through.

The lessons: Touching the heart grounds us. Reminding Charlie of the human side of his life grounded him and enabled him through that lens to see the stereotype he had become. It grounded the mediator who had to let go of his growing desire to see the parties settle, so that the plaintiffs could squarely face the possibility of failure.

Both lawyers and mediators need enough humility to let the parties succeed or fail. The dispute belongs to the parties. Lawyers and mediators sometimes forget this. Lawyers can be transfixed by their advocacy. Mediators may be so focused on securing a settlement, they cannot allow people to fail. Squarely facing failure often triggers a willingness to settle. Many cases which might settle do not.

Another lesson is the power of intentional misleading. Litigators know that much of what they say is intended to mislead the other side. There are serious consequences to this strategy. First, the other side believes it and then the authors may come to believe it themselves.

The mistrust is self-perpetuating. When it reaches a certain point, talks become impossible because no one believes they will help. In this case, the exercise of focusing and clarifying the facts for the mediator led the parties to their own satisfactory resolution in a very short time. The settlement, in excess of $6 million, brought peace to hundreds of workers and a new day to the management of the company. The handshakes at the end were sincere.

A Case Of Trust

Kevin, 17, lived in a foster home with three other boys and Mary, his foster mother. It was two weeks until his trial for attempted murder. He had been snarling at the other boys and Mary as well as not showing up for meals and generally breaking house agreements. The situation was tense and Mary had been told that if things did not improve, Kevin would be moved to another home. She did not want him to go, but couldn't talk with him. She asked for mediation to see if there might be an agreement to establish some guidelines for his staying, not really expecting him even to agree to mediate.

Surprisingly, he agreed. He said he had no particular issues to discuss and said almost nothing about his situation. His contribution was limited to one word replies to questions.

The mediation session took place in their home with the other boys relegated to the basement to do homework. Kevin seemed a little uncomfortable with the fact that the mediator was a woman about the same age as his foster mother. The mediator repeatedly assured him she would be impartial and non-judgmental.

The mediator began by asking Kevin again for his issues.

"I dunno."

"Do you mind being here?"

"No." She gave him a chance to change his mind, then turned to Mary.

As Mary's many issues poured out, the mediator neutralized and clustered them so they did not appear as a litany of grievances.

"Your concerns are about not calling when he isn't going to be home for dinner, not doing his home jobs on time and being unavailable when you want to talk. These are communication issues, is that right?" Even so, the mediation seemed unbalanced.

Kevin agreed to the list, which included behavior around the house, with friends, use of drugs and alcohol, angry outbursts, presence at dinner. They started with the least contentious: dinner time.

Kevin rarely came home in time for dinner or called, yet he had been totally reliable about his 7 p.m. curfew.

"Why?"

"I don't want to go to jail."

The mediator spent a lot of time asking him about his activities and intentions as well as the effect the impending court proceeding was having on him. Each time he responded with a single word, a head shake or nod. The mediator gave him many opportunities to reply, pushing him so Mary could understand. Eventually, she asked,

"Am I pushing you too hard?"

"No," he said softly.

The mediator acknowledged his responses through paraphrase and attempted to round out his expressions in order to put together his reasoning in a more coherent fashion. As she proceeded slowly, she would ask,

"Am I putting words in your mouth?"

"No."

She worked hard to understand without appearing to cross-examine.

His interests were in spending as much time as possible with his friends, maximizing his independence, given the very strict curfew, having a little fun and releasing some stress. His demeanor was very subdued at this point. She took his information at face value, knowing that to assume manipulation would have denied him the opportunity to play this one straight. He was clearly terrified of his court date, feeling he would be incarcerated. All he could think of was that court date. Hanging out with his friends was the way he chose to handle it.

When the mediator turned to Mary to determine her concerns about dinner time, it became clear that her primary interest was respect. When asked why she needed an hour's notice that Kevin would not be there for dinner, she couldn't explain. Then Mary shifted. Influenced by Kevin's responses, she was willing to relinquish all other demands, including adequate notification, having the family all together for dinner and being able to provide good food for the boys.

She began to see Kevin's behavior in different terms — not so much disrespectful as self-comforting. Even his explosions made perfect sense. She had been through this sort of thing before with the other boys, but had been deeply hurt by Kevin's apparent total disregard for her and the others. She knew he was in a bad spot; his case was likely to be bumped up to adult court and result in a long sentence if he were convicted. A dedicated and loving parent, Mary had been trying very hard to be supportive.

This shift in Mary was the turning point in the session. She told Kevin she would back off. Her compassion for him overtook all other needs. Taking the pressure off him also took it off herself. The tension in the room evaporated. Mary recognized this was not the time for negotiation, but simply a time to show her love.

As the mediator and Mary talked casually to close off the session, Mary mentioned that Kevin had not provided his lawyer with the list of friends who could testify on his behalf. By now, the mediator had established a good rapport with Kevin and could quiz him safely. She asked him the state of the list. Kevin told her it wasn't finished, that he needed more addresses, more phone numbers. The mediator told him to bring the list.

Kevin returned from the basement with a scrap of paper containing first names, some addresses and a lot of blanks. He allowed the mediator to go over the items one by one, extracting as much information as he could provide, rewriting the list and making another list of those he needed to call for more information. He placed calls as they all sat there, but needed to catch some people at a different time.

Kevin needed more information about four key people. He said he would do this the next day around dinner time. He was starting a part-time job for the Christmas holidays the next day and wouldn't have time to call the information over to the lawyer. The lawyer urgently needed the information to get the defense together.

Mary said, "I'll call for you, Kevin." Kevin hesitated for a moment and then handed her the list. The mediator sensed the drama, but did not understand it until Mary explained later in private. "Kevin has never before told me the names of his friends or anything about them. They were involved together in drug deals. What he gave me was his list of contacts."

The lesson: The trust built in the mediation allowed Kevin to let down the guard that separated him from everyone, even his loving and dedicated foster mother, when he badly needed help. The mediator built rapport with Kevin by keeping him in control of her understanding. It would have been easy but destructive to pump him for information. Fleshing out his replies as she checked with him to see if her understanding was correct allowed him to control what she knew and to remain silent. Slowly, in this fashion the mediator drew out his underlying interests. The bottom line was that a young man who had gone far toward destroying his life was offered and accepted the chance to win the support of his foster-mother while "playing it straight."

Conclusion

Both of these stories demonstrate something of the transformative power of mediation. People coming to mediation are often stuck. Discussions, if any, have proved fruitless. Parties mired in their one-sided view of the matter continue to see it in the same old way. They are often emotionally stuck as well. A new perspective is needed for the situation to change.

Mediation allows the interplay of timing and sensitivity to bring out the best in people, allaying their fears. With Charlie, it enabled him to become more himself and in turn more sensitive to his client's needs and how to satisfy them. With Mary, it allowed her to see that by helping Kevin meet his needs, hers, too, would be met.

3.
STRATEGIES FOR WAR AND PEACE

Better to be quarreling than lonesome.
— Irish proverb

The Groundwork Of Litigation

"Lit-think" is an attitude that has quietly taken over our consciousness in this century, both individually and societally. It is reflected in such bumper stickers as, "Hit me, I need the money." It drives us to lawyers for advice on everyday business affairs. More than we think, it arises from our emotional response to what we read and hear.

The source of lit-think. Lit-think is based on fear. We fear that we won't get our share, that we'll be taken advantage of, that we'll lose something of great value to us. Businesses act on the same principles.

Fear is pervasive in our society, exposed as it is to violence.[1] If we did not fear that someone would sue us, we would not increase our liability insurance and curtail our operations down to what the carriers consider "safe." Insurance, intended to make us feel safe, seems at times to confirm the reality of our fears.[2]

If we did not fear that we might not get our share, we might not sue a doctor over a relative's death or sue our architect or engineer because we didn't get a perfect house. We don't expect someone we meet everyday on the street to be perfect and we don't sue them unless we're willing to live with the consequences for many years.

Litigation places a barrier between the parties to a dispute which impedes the humanizing of the dispute. Lit-think keeps us stuck in our own view of the situation without having to consider what reasonableness there might be on the other side. The following case illustrates how lit-think kept the parties from resolving a very costly dispute in the early stages.

Case example: lit-think. The corporate owner of a solid waste landfill in Colorado wanted a gas-cleaning plant, to recover fuel from the decomposing waste and help lower the cost of operating the landfill. Its divisional manager found a reputable engineering firm and a deal was struck. The plant was built, but didn't function.

As the dispute escalated, the divisional manager and plant's advocate quit. His successor and the rest of management scrambled for cover, pointing fingers at the contractor to explain why this multi-million dollar investment wasn't working. None of the corporation's executives had a personal stake in the plant's success.

Representatives from both sides met. Accusations flew. Then there was another meeting. By this time, the corporate owner had decided to renege and sought legal advice on how to avoid paying for the construction of the plant. It came into the meeting seeking not the benefit of the contract, but the cheapest way out. It wanted the contractor to absorb the cost of the plant it considered a total loss.

The contractor's management thought the plant was well-designed and constructed. Its investigation showed that the problem was a change in the type of waste being dumped at the landfill — something for which it had not been engineered. They believed the plant could be made to work and wanted to talk about how, not about how much they should pay for what they saw as the client's problems. Not surprisingly, the discussions went nowhere.

A couple of years into the litigation, the owner decided to invite the contractor to mediated discussions. In just two days, the two parties negotiated a settlement that would save each side hundreds of thousands of dollars.

In the beginning, it was easiest to blame the other party. Mediation at that time might have enabled both sides to deal creatively with the situation, saving a fortune.

The owner in this situation acted in a way that was adverse to the deal, justifying it on the ground that the other side was preparing for litigation. This is an example of lit-think. Since the contractor was always trying to make the system work, this justification was in fact only the owner's projection.

Action taken "to protect ourselves" is often adverse to the deal or the relationship. It makes resolution of the problem very unlikely. Rarely do we question our assumptions about the base motives of the other side. It's comforting for a while to rationalize that our destructive actions are okay because the other side is doing the same. But the pleasure doesn't last. We need either to verify those assumptions or abandon them. Even if the other side is behaving offensively, we still need to evaluate the consequences of proceeding with full adversarial steam, because we're very likely to settle, eventually, anyway. Much of our effort and resources will have been wasted.

The Groundwork of Mediation

The cornerstone of mediation is the awareness that in all likelihood the matter in question *will* settle. To resolve early, through negotiation, is the most rational decision, unless for some reason you do not want to resolve, even on terms that are satisfactory to you. See section, "When is it unwise to mediate?" in Chapter 7.

If the matter is not yet in litigation, focus on drawing together what is needed to have a reasoned discussion about resolving (see Fig 2). Do a preliminary investigation, looking possibly toward a joint investigation. You know that informa-

Targeting Agreement

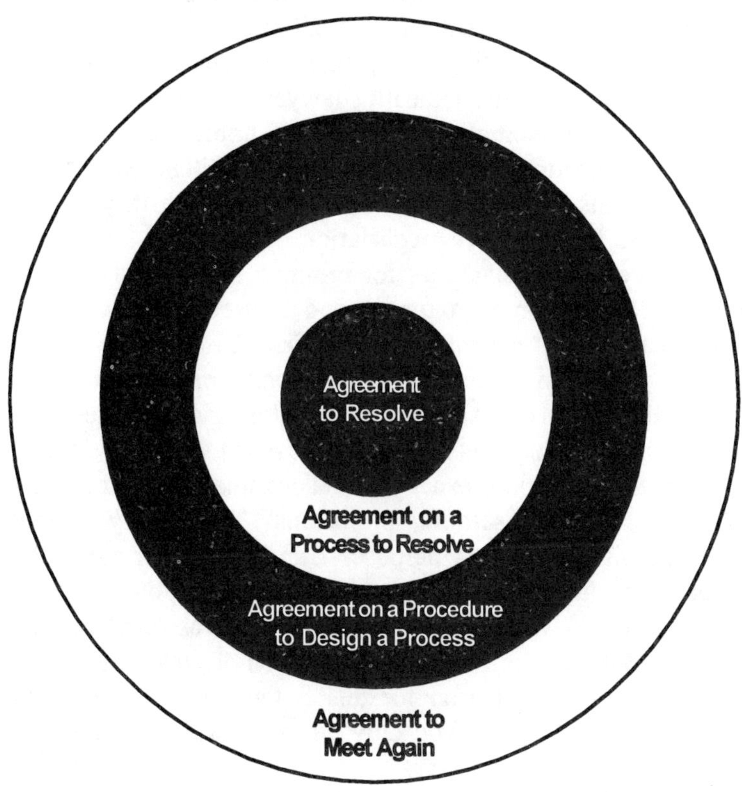

Fig. 2 Steps in resolving disputes (Interaction Associates)

tion gathered jointly will have much more acceptability to the other side. You might want to gather important documents and check the financial impact of what has happened or threatens to happen. Assess your emotional involvement as well, recognizing that anger and fear narrow perspective and get in the way of productive discussions. Plan how to manage these emotions so that you can be more effective in your efforts to resolve your disputes.[3]

You may consult with a lawyer about what information will be needed to secure a satisfactory negotiated resolution. You and your lawyer may consult with a mediator about the steps to take to resolve through mediation.

If the matter is in litigation, case management planning is already taking place. Periodically, lawyers and clients meet to discuss the case, sometimes for a half hour, sometimes for days. These meetings usually focus only on litigation strategy. The discussions will be far more productive when they lay the groundwork for effective negotiation.

Here are a few techniques for bringing an unruly lawsuit to negotiated resolution in a timely and cost-effective way.

• *Do the most critical discovery first.* Discovery, you will recall, is the name given to formal information-gathering tools used in litigation: depositions, interrogatories and requests for production of documents. Analyze proposed discovery activities from the viewpoint, exactly how does this help you and the other side evaluate settlement options? What do you need from this witness for this purpose? Can you get an agreement to get more later, if need be? How strong is that expert's opinion and how will he or she stand up to cross-examination?

The tendency in litigation has been to take important depositions last. The reason for this is the rule, known as the "one bite rule," that says you only get one crack at a non-party witness, without an agreement to the contrary. You don't want to depose a key witness until you know all the questions you want to ask, if you can only depose them once. You can get around this by negotiating for agreements with opposing counsel and the witnesses themselves, if need be. If I were the deponent, I might be happy to agree to a short deposition now at the price of a longer one, maybe, later. The willingness to cooperate should come as no surprise, yet it is rarely sought.

• *Be passionate in pursuing negotiated resolution.* Remember your goal: to settle does not mean to compromise. To settle is to resolve. Its how you settle that determines whether you gave up something of value.

If the opposing party stonewalls, bide your time. There will be opportunities to penetrate the facade through court status conferences and informally at depositions. Repetition alone may win the day. Strategic discussions occurring in the fleeting moments when you can relate to an opposing party or counsel primarily as a human being can win agreement to your approach, for it will be heard with new ears.

Sometimes, courts adopt programs to force early discovery as a means of accelerating the movement of cases to trial. This is the opposite of what a negotiation focus would dictate. The California Fast Track program, like so many rule-driven reforms, has proven itself the litigator's friend.[4]

In the "tracked" cases, parties plunge into vigorous discovery to meet court timetables, long before they know whether or not it is necessary. A study of the San Diego bar's experience under fast track shows there was an explosive growth in area law firms to meet the vastly increased demand for foot soldiers in the discovery wars. Overnight, many major Los Angeles firms that until then had bypassed San Diego set up or merged with local offices.[5]

Equally sad is the fate of "untracked" cases. Courtrooms are made available to fast-track cases by dropping from the calendar a large group of pending cases, such as those filed within one to three years before institution of the program. It can take two years or more to get back on the trial calendar. Meanwhile, momentum to settle vanishes.[6]

Wherever the court has taken an interest in hurrying cases to resolution, your best interests lie in seeking the court's support for your efforts to resolve through mediation.[7] Judges are more and more throwing their support behind voluntary mediation. Unless they detect a purpose to subvert the rules, they will do all they can to help you. Agree to pinpointed discovery, if any at all, and try to postpone the rest while you try to negotiate a resolution.

Negotiate in mediation for the information you need. Instead of written interrogatories, convene a mediated discussion between principals and/or experts. In such discussions, it is possible to greatly narrow the range of issues and broaden the areas of agreement. This type of mediation may be co-mediated. For example, a traditional mediator, charged with keeping the process on track, may work with a technical co-mediator, charged with putting the resulting questions, agreements and output of the process into terms that make sense from a technical point of view.

For safety and simplicity, it is helpful not to give the mediator two roles. When the mediator is also the technical expert, it is much easier to lose trust as the differences between parties become more intense: once the mediator takes a position opposing one or another party, she may lose effectiveness as a neutral.

While mediated discovery may not yield an overall settlement, it will have saved significant time and money. Trustworthiness of information need not be an issue. You can satisfy yourself as to completeness and authenticity by gaining agreement that the information will be provided under a declaration "under penalty of perjury," the way authenticity is assured in discovery.[8]

• *Avoid a battle of the experts.* Another important step in preparing a matter for negotiated resolution is to control the utilization of experts. Mediated negotiations may secure neutral expert opinion right from the beginning.

To secure an agreement for use of a neutral expert, there are many points to negotiate. It is difficult to hold this complex a negotiation together outside the protection of mediation, for it is all too easy to get suspicious of the other side's motives. Nevertheless, it can be done and produce great savings of expense and time. First, the parties share the expert's cost. Second, a neutral expert is more likely to persuade than an opposing party's expert.

See Figure 3 for a checklist of questions covering most issues both sides might want to consider in negotiating for a neutral expert.

NEUTRAL EXPERT CHECKLIST

- what qualifications are needed in the expert?
- by what method will you select the expert?
- who, specifically, will have contact with the expert?
- are the other parties entitled to know what each has communicated to the expert?
- shall the expert be able to investigate outside of his contact with the parties?
- with whom may the expert talk?
- should you decide just what the expert is to be told about the underlying dispute and if so, what?
- what provision will be made to check on the expert's progress to be sure the work is on track?
- what kind of report does the expert need to produce?
- what can be done with the expert's opinion?
- can the expert be used by any party, in the event adjudication is required?

Fig. 3 Checklist

It's a little frightening to send a neutral expert out to investigate something when you have no idea how it will turn out. What if the expert comes out against you? Well, that's life. What better time to know your problems than early on? What you risk, if the expert is wrong and against you, is that the other side gets a bit too cocky. That's nothing new and you have tools for dealing with that. What you gain is an opportunity to sell your view of the situation through an expert who has the ear of opposing counsel and the opposing party, whom you must persuade in order to succeed through negotiation.

• *Manage the case strategically.* Focusing on securing a negotiated resolution defines the environment in which all activity takes place; this strategy will fail, however, if you neglect it when litigation activity grows intense.

Organizations are composed of shifting power groups. In opposing an organization, we need to cultivate those groups which favor a resolution we would find acceptable. We want to enlarge their voice in the decision-making structure of the opposing party organization. This helps secure satisfactory results by keeping us from making a devil out of our opponent and keeps alive the possibility of serious settlement talks.

Most people are familiar with the "good guy, bad guy" style of managing contacts with the opposing party. Tactics for handling that gambit are discussed in Fisher and Ury's *Getting To Yes* under the heading of "dirty tricks." Such games often serve merely to block meaningful communications. A good counter-strategy is to name the game, bringing it out in the open. For example, "You seem to be using good guy-bad guy tactics here. I don't believe that's helpful." Such games are a symptom of dysfunctional communication: no one's really listening; each is taking a role, wearing a mask.

Managing a case for early negotiated resolution requires finesse. Everything that happens or that fails to happen presents an opportunity to plant the seed of an idea, to assess the situation and strategize anew. In this work, mediation, not litigation, is the better tool.

Notes to Chapter 3

1. See, for example, "The Violence Among Us," a speech by Bernd Huppauf, professor of German at New York University, at the conference on "Violence, War and Modern Memory," at N.Y.U. October, 1993, reported in the *New York Times*, Op-Ed, Nov. 21, 1993, p. E17. He notes: "The dividing line between ourselves and those whom we fear is an illusion: violence is as much a part of each of us as it is a part of our society."

2. The insurance companies are not the enemy. Carriers work on calculated margins and long-term contracts to manage the risk

they assume. Initially, insurance was sold cheap, with sales promoted by telling people all the horrible things that *could* (but hadn't) happened. Now it all has happened, which means very high premiums as underwriters speculate on what will happen in the future. Insurance today protects us from litigation while by its nature encouraging litigation through the presence of readily available cash. Fifty years or so ago, a prospective plaintiff had to contemplate first winning a lawsuit, then forcing a defendant to pay, by perhaps losing his business, his house and perhaps his family and his life. At that time, community values did not encourage litigation.

In the United States today, the insurance industry feels besieged by ever-broader liability and larger judgments. Yet its commitment to using mediation is still weak — Aetna Life & Casualty Insurance Co., for example, estimates that only ten percent of lawsuits go to mediation. Yet mediation spells major relief from litigation costs. By embracing collaborative problem-solving, carriers could do much to discourage a flight to the courts of more and more disputes with wider and wider sweeps of liability.

3. See Appendix 1, *Decompression Exercise*, for a technique useful in detaching from the emotional freight that comes with most disputes, allowing one to regain perspective.

4. The burden of Fast Track is its requirement that litigants promptly initiate discovery activity that may well prove necessary. See n. 5.

5. The San Diego Bar Association, a voluntary organization, saw an increase in the *rate of growth* in memberships of about 18%, in the period 1988-1989 and a decline of about 75%, again in the rate, in 1990-1991 (conversation with Julie Haig, Executive Director, San Diego Bar Association, October 27, 1993). See also Marilyn Huff, *Fast Track: Reduces Court Delay*, J. Contemp. Legal Issues, 1989, pp. 222-227, relating complaints from various attorneys, including plaintiffs' lawyers who "say their caseload is many times higher than defense attorneys' caseload because the plaintiff attorneys try to settle the case with the insurance carrier before the complaint is filed," at p. 225. Ms. Huff, now U.S. District Court Judge, related also that, "The institution of Fast-Track has meant full employ-

ment for court reporters," at p. 224.

The Fast Track program has reduced delay in many California courts. It has done so, however, at the cost of forcing discovery to take place *before the parties decide it is needed.* This benefits defense lawyers, who are usually paid by the hour, but hurts plaintiffs' lawyers, whose own funds often finance litigation costs for clients. Whatever the benefits of Fast Track for the courts, it has been no boon to clients, although this seems to be fairly well-hidden from the courts, who measure success in time to disposition.

6. Initiation of a Fast Track Program is a good time to lure the dropped cases into mediation. Mediators create a sense of urgency about settlement, at times getting the parties to agree at the outset that "this is it," and by keeping the pressure on the parties to live up to that commitment. If at the end of the day there is no settlement and no information the parties feel they need to evaluate settlement options, the decision not to settle is likely to be a well-thought-out decision to try the case.

7. See "Case example, Winning the Judge's Support," in Chapter 9.

8. In litigation, authenticity in answers to interrogatories and productions of documents used to be assured by a notarized statement that the information was true and correct or complete. Over the past decade, most jurisdictions have changed to the declaration under penalty of perjury, which does essentially the same thing but does not need a notary public.

PART 2

Obstacles to Resolving

To quote from Pogo, "We have found the enemy and it is us." How many times have we come to the end of a blind alley, realizing that it was not the opposition but our own weaknesses and mistakes which did us in? How can we learn to see these as they are developing?

4.
SELF-MADE STUMBLING BLOCKS

Finally, you understand that the real motorcycle you're working on is yourself.
— Robert M. Pirsig in *Zen and the Art of Motorcycle Maintenance*

In our less rational moments, we might willingly hurt ourselves in order to hurt another. Not infrequently, litigation is pursued with such self-destructive motives. Not until the end do we discover how much the exercise really cost us.

A story is told in Russia of a farmer who was plowing one day when he accidently captured a genie.[1] He was given one wish, "But, whatever you get," the genie said, "your neighbor will receive double." The farmer thought for a long time. "Blind me in one eye," he said.

A major difficulty in securing cost-effective legal representation is our societal approach to the lawyer-client relationship. Problems arise because often clients are not clear about what they want to accomplish. They hold on to fantasies: cost-free vengeance or thinking they want something done now (a near impossibility in the tangled world of the legal system). When they finally get focused on what really can be accomplished, they get more reasonable and therefore get better results. In a sense, the litigation waltz is usually no more than an elaborate ritual to get litigants to tap into that part of themselves that knows what their long-term interests are and what it takes to serve them.

In *New World, New Mind* Paul Ehrlich and Robert Ornstein show how the mind that served primitive humans so well over the millennia utterly fails to help us cope with today's world. People filter information so as to make it manageable and reduce it to caricatures, to a sort of mental shorthand. They respond quickly to sudden change but hardly at all to gradual change.

One of the reasons why Americans have put up with over-litigation as long as we have is simply because we are habituated to it. For most of the past 25 years, we no longer questioned the delay and expense and inconvenience. These conditions were a given. Today, it is the old brain which holds mediation at bay, insisting that prolonged but customary litigation activity take place first.

How We Have Kept Mediation At Bay

There are certain things some of us just cannot accept. Chief among them is change. As Lewis Carroll put it in *Through the LookingGlass*,

> "I can't believe that," said Alice. "Can't you," the Queen said in a pitying tone. "Try again: draw a long breath and shut your eyes." Alice laughed. "There's no use trying," she said. "One can't believe impossible things." "I dare say you haven't had much practice," said the Queen. "When I was younger, I always did it for half an hour a day. Why sometimes, I've believed as many as six impossible things before breakfast."

Many of the rationalizations used to put off or avoid mediation ignore the reality that mediation excels at dealing with just such concerns.

1. **This matter won't settle. The other side is too unreasonable and there is too much hostility.**
   Mediation is a process in which both sides are encouraged to be more reasonable and less hostile. A mediator may be able

to discover why previous efforts at settlement failed and to devise solutions.

2. **I've settled many matters before, without ever needing a mediator.**
   It is true that in the long run, almost all disputes settle. The question is when, how well and at what cost.

3. **We don't need to settle this case. If I wanted to settle, I would just call the other side.**
   It is always possible to lose in court or to get less than you deserve. In mediation, you can at least find out what your choices are. You may still decide not to resolve, but it will be an informed decision.

4. **Why mediate? We have a mandatory settlement conference with a judge coming up soon.**
   Mandatory settlement conferences with a judge are often too brief to help. In many, there is pressure to settle. Mediators have been trained in communication and settlement techniques most judges are unfamiliar with.

5. **This dispute is too complex for mediation.**
   Mediation works extremely well in complex cases because each item can be negotiated separately or as part of a whole package. Also, it is much easier to untangle complex situations where what we are doing is problem-solving. And if the matter cannot be settled, it has at least been simplified and made less costly.

6. **We don't trust the other party. They've not acted in good faith.**
   Mediation is a process in which remedies can be created that do not depend on trust — for example, one side's performance can be contingent on completion of an act by the other side; authenticity and completeness can be sworn to under penalty of perjury. Trust is destroyed by the adversarial nature of

litigation, but is often restored in mediation, by the nature of the process.

7. **We've completed discovery and a trial date is set. Why should we mediate?**
   In mediation when both sides agree, both have won. And they have laid the groundwork for a peaceable future relationship, however distant. At trial we may still lose, for despite discovery, there may be some surprises.

8. **Mediation will only provide the other side with an opportunity for free discovery.**
   Each side has control over how much information it discloses in mediation. Both sides will learn more about each other's case in mediation, but the truth will come out at trial anyway. Surprises do not necessarily help or produce fair results.

9. **Since this is a non-binding process, there is nothing to keep the parties from changing their minds.**
   When mediation results in agreement, a document is prepared which makes the settlement final and binding. It sticks because the parties are invested in it. Before agreement, the parties have a right to change their minds, to try an option out, or make sure the final result feels balanced and fair.

10. **The only way to teach the other side a lesson is to get a court judgment.**
    You may be right. But it is often we who end up being taught the lesson, because of what it costs us to get that result. Only later may we realize that we could have done as well or better in a negotiation.[2]

Perspectives: Ours And Others

We often lose perspective when it is our ox that has been gored. People whom we have dealt with for years take on a sinister look; we project our own anger on them and then are frightened by what we see. We take their angry words literally and convince ourselves that when they speak softly, it is for devious purposes. We overestimate their destructive capabilities, in part to justify our own adversarial buildup.

When I was in college, a rosy-cheeked, robust, good-looking CPA graduate student was convicted of the brutal rape/murder of another student. On the eve of his execution, the newspaper portrait of him showed a man with thin lips, dark shadows under his eyes and a sickly look. It later emerged that the photo had been retouched to make the attractive young man look evil, perhaps to make the public happier with the execution.

In disputes, we do much the same thing with our minds. We no longer see the "enemy" as we did before the dispute arose. The mere thought of them makes us tense or angry.

The other side sees us in much the same way. Hears us in much the same way. Projects on us in much the same way. Ignores what we're really saying in much the same way.

Restoring balance to perspective. Distorted perception adds immeasurably to the burdens of the situation. Nevertheless, there is a certain satisfaction we derive from feeling right. To regain balance, we need to be willing to let that go. That does not mean letting go of our claim or defense or weakening our will in any way. It means letting go of the victim-stance, of the pleasure of feeling wronged.

Regaining balance may require only a few quiet minutes' work with a professional counselor. Most of us find it hard to dispel the emotional side effects of disputing. We become so stressed, it impacts our day-to-day lives. A do-it-yourself approach is laid out in Appendix 1, *Decompression Exercise*. Such clearing is sometimes called forgiveness work. It does not mean condoning or making okay something that was definitely not okay. It means separating what others have done from what we are doing to ourselves now by holding on to destructive emotions about what they did. We give up the sour satisfaction of holding another responsible in order to secure the far greater pleasure of reclaiming power to get results in the situation.

For example, when I hold my mother responsible for not providing me with a good maternal model, I inhibit my own ability to be the best mother I can be. I blind myself to the qualities and habits in myself that I dislike in her, making it impossible for me to change into the kind of person I want to be. When you hold anger toward a former partner over a financial debacle in the partnership, you blind yourself to your own contribution to the situation, making it more likely you will repeat the pattern.

You may ask, what good is it to regain a balanced perspective, when others may remain distorted in their perceptions? Simple. Once we are clear, we become far more creative and far more effective in moving the situation toward a resolution that serves us. This helps to clear the other side's perceptions as well.

Until we clear our perception, we are likely to hurt ourselves more than others could. With even a modest emotional burden, we are likely to stir up unnecessary legal work for which we pay, one way or another. We may snarl and sulk around, or play Camille, the eternal victim, for the next few years. There are endless variations. In either state of mind, mediation seems unappealing. So we add to our problems rather than resolving them.

Rage appears empowering while, in fact, it only holds us hostage. We may be powerful in blocking another's path, but we are usually powerless to get a result that works for us. A balanced perspective allows us to lighten up, to regain personal power and effectiveness. And it allows us to see the advantages of mediating.

Tools that bite. The heavier the emotional charge on the dispute, the more likely we are to use high-risk negotiating strategies, when we finally do decide to negotiate or mediate. These tend to defeat negotiations and make a mockery of mediation. Two examples are:

• *Secrecy and deception.* People conceal or misrepresent their preferences and priorities when they believe that if the other side knew their true desires, they would *never* get satisfaction. It is a marketplace strategy expected to lead the merchant to offer a lower price. However, this technique may prevent the other side from offering the very thing we most want. Discussions become more a performance than a negotiation.[3]

• *Intransigence.* Refusing to move is a strategy often based on fear,[4] the belief that moving off of a fixed position shows too much interest in resolving, for example. It is a refusal to negotiate which passes up the opportunity to resolve *now*. It invites retaliation, which means an end to the discussions.

Attitudes That Impede Resolution

Certain attitudes also reduce our ability to satisfy our interests through negotiation and mediation. They usually function undetected just below our awareness.

• *Asking for more than satisfaction.* Sometimes we reject options that meet our interests because we think the other side is "gaining more or losing less" than they should. If something satisfies our interests, it is sufficient, whether or not the other side got its "just desserts." To hold otherwise is to subordinate our self-interest to our desire to hurt the other.

• *Loss aversion.* Sometimes we focus so intently on not losing anything, we undervalue our gains. The arms negotiations provide an example. American arms negotiators often felt that what the Russians offered to give up wasn't worth nearly as much as what they asked us to give up. Since we always had substantially greater military capability than the Russians, this attitude was self-defeating. It took years to reach an agreement that might more readily have been reached in the absence of loss aversion.

• *Believing our own puff.* When we are out of balance, the mere fact that we are offering to give something up may cause us to become much more attached to that item. The old, yellow, cat-clawed sofa that wouldn't bring $50 at a yard sale becomes a valuable "antique," after we've offered to let our nearly ex-spouse have it. This is seen as dishonest by the other side and heightens distrust. It is particularly destructive when *both* sides are doing it.

• *Knee-jerk reactivity.* Often, we dismiss proposals which

might serve our interests quite well, just because the other side made them. Studies confirm this. In one sidewalk survey, pedestrians were asked to evaluate a hypothetical nuclear disarmament proposal. They were told either that the U.S. proposed it, that the Russians proposed it or that a neutral third party proposed it. Reactions were highly favorable when it was attributed to the U.S., unfavorable when it was attributed to the Russians and in between when it was attributed to a neutral third party.[5]

Needs That Do Not Serve

We also confuse desires based on fear with real needs.[6] We then convince ourselves that nothing will suffice unless these false needs are met. Do any of these sound familiar?

• *The need to control.* Controlling people usually feel they must make the final proposal. They must put forth proposals for the other side to consider, not vice versa. This alienates the other side, pushing it to wrestle for control, also. The antidote to this is to force ourselves to work from the other side's proposals, if no mediator is present. We may also use mediation to mask the originator of proposals, so they may more readily be considered on their merits.

• *The need to be right.* It is difficult to accept now what we rejected a while ago, even when it makes sense. It is a mark of statesmanship to do it gracefully: "You know, you were right about that. I see what you're driving at." This approach, when sincere, engenders trust and makes it easier to reach overall agreement.

• *The need to keep fighting.* Settling, even when we get 110 percent of what we want, often feels like we're giving something up. We're giving up the dispute, with all that entails. There are payoffs for being a victim; we attract sympathy, or perhaps something more tangible. We give these up for a greater good only when we're ready.

• *The need for vindication.* The rosy view that our day in court will mean that the judge says, "You're right," is largely illusory. There is only a small chance our case will be tried and the there is no guarantee of a clear decision on the merits. The few well-publicized court victories hide legions of the disappointed.[7]

• *The need to be nice.* Often, cordiality masks the real problems, but neither side is willing to risk disturbing the atmosphere in order to see if progress can be made on deeper issues. We may start out being cordial and quickly slide into a real fight, when anger springs up unexpectedly. There is no point in taking that risk, we reason. Mediation allows tougher subjects to be tackled with dignity and without offense. With or without mediation, antagonism is not a necessary part of a dispute.

Accepting responsibility for being part of the problem is a first step in securing resolution, even if we've done nothing else.

Notes to Chapter 4

1. Mediator and former United States Attorney Sidney Lezak of Portland, Oregon, brought this story back from Russia.

2. Thanks to Ken Cloke of the Center for Dispute Resolution in Santa Monica, California and to Jerry Murase for this list.

3. In *Breaking the Impasse, Consensual Approaches to Resolving Public Dispute*, Lawrence Susskind and Jeffrey Cruikshank identify a willingness to exchange accurate information about each side's true priorities as crucial to transforming win-lose disputes into all-gain agreements. Basic Books, 1987, at p. 33.

4. For an interesting vignette about resolving youth gang disputes by recognizing and working with the motivator, fear, see Edelman and Crain, *The Tao of Negotiation,* 1993, pp. 70-72.

5. Much of this discussion is based on the work of Lee Ross and Constance Stillinger, "Barriers to Conflict Resolution," *Negotiation Journal,* Oct., 1991, p. 389 and following. See also Stillinger, Epelbaum,

Keltner & Ross, "The Reactive Devaluation Barrier to Conflict Resolution," *Journal of Personality and Social Psychology*, 1990.

6. For a critique of needs as an interpretive tool for analyzing conflict as developed in the work of John W. Burton (*Resolving Deep-rooted Conflict: A Handbook*, 1987), see Avruch and Black, "Ideas of Human Nature in Contemporary Conflict Resolution Theory," *Negotiation Journal*, July, 1990, at pp. 221, 225, 227.

7. In forgiveness workshops I teach, we explore the physiological and emotional impact of disputing. In one exercise, participants are asked to observe the physical effects of the rage engendered by a situation. They are then asked to imagine that the other side has taken out a full-page ad in the *New York Times* or their local newspaper, saying in effect "I was wrong. You were right. I'm terribly sorry." To date, not one participant has felt any lessening of the rage, in contemplating such an action. This illustrates an important truth: nothing another person does can relieve us of what we choose to cling to.

5.
LAWYERS AT THE THRESHOLD

He who sues my client is my friend.
— Lawyer proverb

In a dispute, we often seek legal counsel. We may have concluded that we have no options except to pursue or defend litigation. Often, this is the last thing we want, yet in the United States it is the first thing we think of doing when other avenues seem closed off. In this chapter, we look at the legal profession for a better understanding of the resource and to see how lawyers relate to mediation.

Lawyers As Soldiers

The genus "lawyer" has come, during much of this century, in roughly two species. One is the transactional lawyer. This lawyer helps structure deals, negotiates and writes contracts for us, and plans our estate.

The other is the advocate. The advocate speaks for us in adversarial forums, such as arbitration or the courts. If we could, we might seek an advocate to work on litigation, and a transactional lawyer to represent us in mediation.[1] Once litigation begins, however, we usually have an advocate. Some lawyers are generalists, true problem-solvers, and are right at home in mediation, regardless of the nature of their day to day practice.

Whoever represents us influences how others involved in the

dispute see us. If our lawyer is arrogant, boorish, or angry, we are taken to be likewise. If our lawyer is dignified, intelligent, responsive and wise, we are presumed to be the same. Advocates often equate themselves to soldiers and litigation to war. In fact, however, litigation is more like a ritual dance leading most of the time to a negotiated resolution. Like tribal dancers, lawyers put on giant masks and costumes and ritually fight each other, using not sticks and magic hoops, but acres of trees neatly pressed into paper. They fight with words as if only their adversary's death itself would amount to victory. Yet they settle before the final act. Litigation is much more like theater than war.

The kind of lawyer we use has a lot to do with the quality of our experience in resolving disputes. Soldier lawyers are often aggressive and take upon themselves authority they should not have. When the soldier lawyer determines what is to be won, how it is to be won and what costs and what delays are acceptable he becomes his own client. He wages the battle for his own glory, or his own economic gain instead of yours. And he invites problems of professional behavior and ethics as well as major problems with perspective.

Client Control: An Evolving Concept

A phrase commonly used by lawyers, particularly in the past, is "client control."[2] Not so long ago, a lawyer who did not have client control — that is, the lawyer speaking for the client, without more than a perfunctory approval process — was much looked down upon by other lawyers. When applied to procedural agreements, client control affirmed that the lawyer was properly vested with authority.

The concept of client control has, however, also been used in settlement negotiations. Lawyers may agree to resolve a matter without talking with the client, before the client even knows discussions might take place. Often these "discussions" are very, very brief. The idea that the case is the client's and not the lawyer's hasn't always been accepted, but it is clear that clients are entitled to be consulted about the settlement of their cases. Increasingly, "client control" is coming to mean the *client* is in control. This new relationship requires that the client take more responsibility for what happens in the course of the representation.

Mediation puts us back into a position of control, participating actively or passively in joint and confidential discussions. There has been plenty of opportunity to assess options and agreement is only reached if it is acceptable to us. As a result of the mediation, we have a better understanding of the range of realistic settlements.

Mediation fits with today's greater recognition of ethical standards concerning the limits of legal representation.[3] It satisfies the lawyer's ethical responsibility to sufficiently inform us so that we may make sound decisions.

By contrast, when only lawyers participate in the negotiations, settlement possibilities can be presented to us with what seem to be strings attached. For example, lawyers at times threaten to resign from the matter if their recommendations are not taken. Sometimes a lawyer needs to withdraw, because she will have lost effectiveness. But whatever lawyers do, they are required to act consistently with the client's interest.[4]

To decide what kind of outcomes meet our true interests, we need a serious talk with our lawyer. Trying to talk to a soldier about long-term interests is often futile. For such discussions, we need a counselor-at-law, worthy of the name.

Lawyers As Counselors-at-law

A counselor helps us clarify our objectives, decide what resources to commit to pursuing them and assess how much delay can be tolerated. A good counselor-at-law will find what our real interests are — beyond our stated goals, which are often very short-term — and devise realistic options to serve our best interests. Like a skilled coach, this lawyer helps us regain our balance and effectiveness.

The personal injury plaintiff's lawyer has even greater need to be such a counselor. The client's suffering may be so severe, the disruption of his or her life so traumatic, and the consequences of losing so terrible, that decisions about handling the matter and about seeking and evaluating settlement options are major life decisions for the client. Keeping the client well-informed in a considerate way and respecting the client's need to make the key decisions are all part of the work of the lawyer-counselor.

The business lawyer also needs to be a counselor. Organizational clients often have political problems. This is as true for labor unions and churches as it is for corporations. As counselor, the lawyer may be called upon to help keep the group functional while seeking direction for the handling of legal matters. For example, some clients refuse to suggest mediation because they believe the other side would reject their overtures. The lawyer might want to secure an offer to mediate from the other side, so that his own clients would be able to consider the option from a fresh viewpoint.

Lawyers As Storytellers

Good negotiators are storytellers. The lawyer as storyteller first listens very carefully to her client. When put together by the storyteller, the story is not likely to accuse others of wrongdoing so much as to raise questions. The storyteller understands that only a minimal amount of involvement or intention is required to establish or rebut a legal claim. The fact that we may well be accusatorial at trial does not mean that we need to be that way in day to day contacts. It just makes people hard to deal with.

The lawyer as storyteller sees the steps leading up to a trial as a series of opportunities to enlarge acceptance of his client's story by the court, the opposing party and opposing counsel. Little by little, the story will be refined to include as much of the other side's story as it can, narrowing the areas of disagreement.

At each step of the way in mediation, counsel decides what, if anything, to disclose and how to disclose it. This moment-by-moment decision-making is the forte of the lawyer as storyteller, for in storytelling, timing is everything. It is the storyteller who can redirect the energy from oppositional channels into problem-solving channels.

How Does Mediation Impact Lawyers?

Counsel who serve their clients as problem-solvers rather than problem-massagers will spend a lot less time on any given matter. This runs counter to the revenue-generating demands of many law firms, which cause each new case to be viewed according to its predicted contribution to the income stream.[5] Standard case-handling procedures often require sufficient legal work to make this prediction come true, except for firms working primarily on a contingent fee basis, for whom economy of effort is key.

With notable exceptions, many law firms look to the client for the motivation to resolve early without all of that legal work.[6] Some realize, however, that effective and efficient legal services and satisfied clients will produce more business with the potential for higher per unit compensation for lawyers, as productivity rises. Indeed, some disputes that currently fester unresolved because of the costs and delay may find their way to lawyers skilled in mediation and other alternatives to litigation.

Value is a major focus among heavy consumers of legal services, such as corporations. Value refers to what it costs us to resolve the dispute. It is the antithesis of hourly billing, which has dominated the profession for a generation.[7] Value-added is becoming a watchword among lawyer-watchers, as the profession moves to alter the decades-old pattern of basing fees on time spent rather than results achieved.

The story is told about the cruise ship that set sail from New York to London some years back. A boiler broke down and the ship could only move forward at a very slow speed. On board was a master ship's mechanic who offered his services for his usual fee. The captain quickly took him up on it. He went to the boiler room, examined the boiler and piping, took a large wrench and twisted one valve. It was quickly apparent that the problem was solved. Later the shipping company received a bill for $2,050. When it inquired about the charge, the reply was: "$50 is for my time. $2,000 is for knowing what to do."

The legal system has not been known for encouraging the

reforms that make lawyers and litigation more efficient. Many reforms spring from the belief that the courts can take better care of litigants than lawyers can. The California Fast Track system, for example, makes extensive use of forms that are time-consuming to complete and of rigid time-tables backed up by sanctions. Such procedural requirements may be expensive. Voluntary mediation has always been efficient and considerate of parties. It loses some of that efficiency, however, when it is mandatory and then gets too dragged out.[8] A client willing to pay for results rather than the expenditure of metered time, stands to save significantly.

How Do Lawyers Impact Mediation?

All counsel are usually involved in mediation if one counsel is. This is because lawyers are under ethical constraints about talking directly to other parties who have lawyers. These can be waived by the non-attending lawyer, but must otherwise be respected. Blanket waivers are made under certain circumstances, such as when a party's negotiator is a lawyer. In many insurance mediations, the claims professional does not have counsel present, even though the plaintiff or claimant usually does. Also, where one counsel is especially trusted by opposing counsel, his participation will not necessarily draw in all the others.

There are risks to negotiating without counsel. Among them is the risk of being a less-experienced negotiator than the other parties. Or we may be desperate to settle and give up too much, thinking it necessary to reach agreement. We also may be blind to the weaknesses of our position or the strength of the other side's position, leading us to take ridiculous positions, because we are too close to the situation. There are times, particularly in relationship negotiations, when one party is incapable of negotiating. In marital mediation, it is usually but not always the woman. It may be the man — perhaps a former combat soldier struggling to live a normal life — who simply withdraws, feeling unable to fight without inflicting unacceptable wounds. Without adequate representation mediation is not an option in such situations.

On the other hand, there are times when party negotiation

makes sense. If one or more counsel have been the source of friction, the other counsel may encourage his client to talk directly to the other side, taking himself out of the picture in order to take the opposing counsel out as well. Each situation must be evaluated on its own merits.

Even if not present, counsel can inform client and mediator about desirable formulations for any settlement agreement. Not infrequently, counsel who have been on the sidelines during a mediation will come forward at the conclusion to memorialize the agreement until the formal documents are prepared.

Once the dispute reaches the problem-solving stage, counsel serve by seeing that reasonable agreements are reached and that they are secure, safe from disruption caused by subsequent counsel review or some facet that was overlooked. Here is where the legal mind and training are of greatest service.

Generally, lawyers are present during the mediation of matters in litigation. If they aren't working effectively together, part of the mediator's work is to make that relationship more functional. When committed to the process, lawyers are an excellent resource. When lawyers don't participate, they may undermine what the parties do in mediation. By overprotection bred from a lack of understanding of the tradeoffs, they spare us a moment's headache so we can enjoy a long-term disability.

How can lawyers make mediation productive? Lawyers can provide a level playing field for the parties in a variety of ways.

• *They can establish a range of outcomes at trial.* This is one of the most constructive uses of a lawyer's expertise and brings the matter down to real life in a hurry. It lets us know what will happen if we don't settle. A lawyer who overestimates a case early in the representation may find it difficult to get the client to buy into a less optimistic outcome when problems emerge. Mediation addresses this dilemma.

The risks of going to court are always significant. There are no guarantees. In order to make a realistic decision to go forward, we need to accept the real possibility of total defeat. This does a lot to reduce surprises. The decision to fight or not to fight is always ours, not the lawyer's. And it is we who must take responsibility for the decision.[9]

Some clients try to waffle on this decision, so as to be able to hold the lawyer responsible if it doesn't work out. That is not the way to get a good decision and we end up mostly hurting ourselves. Lawyers in such a bind can become pretty tough on their clients, forcing them to settle for what is available at the last minute. Clients who can face losing may be less risk averse than counsel, who may want to settle, because they do not want to risk losing at trial the money they have advanced on the case. For other clients, some kind of recovery is crucial. For them, statistics are meaningless. If their case is unsuccessful, it doesn't matter that they had a ninety-nine percent chance of succeeding. Mediation tends to clarify the client's commitment to settlement or trial, once and for all.

• *Lawyers can work out their own differences.* Lawyer animosity in litigated disputes is often high and is always expensive. Civil litigation is often frustrating. We may hear about it when our lawyer complains about how the *other* lawyer is causing all the difficulties and delays. In such situations, focus on ways of reducing the antagonism. One lawyer I know simply went over to an opposing counsel's office one day. After a quiet talk, the opposing lawyer became much less obstructive. It is constructive to take an interest in eliminating unnecessary frictions.

• *They can work with the mediator.* Working together, lawyers and mediators can form an effective team to encourage clients to end their fighting, control difficult personalities and aggressive or violent behavior and start to get on with their lives. In the heat of battle it is not always obvious that one's self-interest includes reaching agreements through collaborative negotiation and compromise. Nothing is more disruptive than the loser who needs to retaliate, robbing the victor of the benefits of victory. A way of avoiding this is to see that everyone wins in some measure, even if the win is very small. The need to retaliate depends on perceived injustice.

In one wrongful termination mediation, it turned out that the plaintiff had no case. A witness was mistaken. The case was set for trial and it would have been costly for the defendant to seek dismissal formally without the plaintiff's cooperation. As part of the settlement here, the defendant paid $200 to help defray the plaintiff's costs. This token settlement led to a final and binding resolution.

Insisting that for us to win, justice requires that the other side must lose, creates a very large hurdle to getting what we want. It is a "war" metaphor not a "peace" metaphor. In order to keep the peace, each side must have something worth protecting, even if it is simply one's self-esteem.

Conclusion. Refusing to mediate until most pre-trial legal work is done robs clients of many of the benefits of mediation. This makes no sense from the client's point of view, except when there is so little information available it is impossible even to lay the groundwork for exploring settlement options.

Lawyers have persisted in this old kind of thinking because clients weren't paying attention. No more.[10] The legal profession is going through profound changes now, and firms are already changing the way they offer their services. The future belongs to those who will solve problems rather than to those who engage in extravagant contests, only, eventually, to resolve through negotiation.

Notes to Chapter 5

1. Not all transactional lawyers are good negotiators. Those who specialize in contracts can be as wedded to words as anyone. As one lawyer put it, "Even three or four words could be the exact focus of later litigation. I'm going to do everything I can to see that my client isn't hurt in that fight, even if the deal suffers." No wonder lawyers are sometimes called "deal-breakers."

2. Clients have been able to nullify settlement agreements reached

without their approval. See "Your Ethical and Fiduciary Obligations in the Settlement of Disputes," R. Clifford Potter, *ALI-ABA Course Materials Journal* vol.15, n. .3, p. 99; ABA Model Rule 1.2(a). See also, Robert F. Cochran, Jr., "Legal Representation and the Next Steps Toward Client Control: Attorney Malpractice for Failure to Allow the Client to Control Negotiation and Pursue Alternatives to Litigation," 47 *Washington and Lee Law Review*, 1990, pp. 819, 823-24.

3. The Model Rules of Professional Conduct were adopted by the American Bar Association in 1983 as an ethical standard for lawyer representation suggested for consideration and adoption by the various states. Rule 1.2 provides:

> A lawyer shall abide by the client's decisions concerning the objective of representation . . . and shall consult with the client as to the means by which they are to be pursued. A lawyer shall abide by a client's decision whether to accept an offer of settlement of a matter. . .

Although these rules are not binding until adopted by the supreme court of the state in which the lawyer practices, they provide a shorthand way of talking about long-established requirements.

4. See note 3.

5. Leonard L. Riskin wrote long ago about the relationship of lawyers to mediation. He states that the lawyer's philosophical map rests primarily on ". . . two assumptions about matters that lawyers handle: 1) disputants are adversaries—i.e., if one wins, the other must lose, and 2) disputes may be resolved through application, by a third party, of some general rule of law." He notes that these two assumptions along with the real demands of the adversary system and the expectations of many clients, tend to exclude mediation from most lawyers' repertoires.

"Lawyers," he argues, "are trained to put people and events into categories that are legally meaningful, to think in terms of rights and duties established by rules, to focus on acts more than persons. This view requires a strong development of cognitive capabilities, which is often attended by the under-cultivation of emotional faculties. This combination of capacities [tends to cause lawyers] either to reduce most nonmaterial values to amounts of money or to sweep them under the carpet. . ." Riskin, "Mediation and Lawyers," 43 *Ohio State Law Journal,* 1982, pp. 29, 43-48, 57-59.

6. Steven Brill uses *The American Lawyer* to herald changes in the way law is practiced. In "Headnotes: The New Leverage" he celebrates a Houston law firm for its value-based billing and staffing policies. The firm's policy is "to make money on our work, not on our hours." "Our rates ($300 per hour for a lawyer of 13 years' experience) are high, but ... our bills are low," observed one partner in the firm. The firm's flexible pricing schedule includes a kicker for results, where possible. See chapter 1, note 1. See also, LaMothe, "Opening Statement: Thinking of Mediation," *Litigation Journal ,19*:4, Summer, 1993, at p. 1. And see Darlene Ricker, The Vanishing Hourly Fee," *American Bar Association Journal,* March, 1994, at p. 66, for a good description of how law firms are testing alternative billing approaches, under client pressure.

7. See *Beyond the Billable Hour,* Richard C. Reed, ed., ABA Section of Economics of Law Practice, 1989, an anthology issued by the Special Task Force on lawyer fees and billing. The various alternative billing approaches are discussed, also, in "The Vanishing Hourly Fee." See n. 6, above.

8. Court-mandated mediation again gives rise to special problems. For example, in one jurisdiction, construction cases are routinely referred to a single special master for discovery management and settlement mediation. This has given him a virtual monopoly and counsel report that it has also materially increased the cost of handling these cases, where settlement is not readily achieved. After the parties have given settlement their best shot, they still have to drag through settlement exercises, often involving a lot of expert time and expense. This may end up costing them more than if the case were tried.

   Some cases need to be tried. By keeping the mediation voluntary, the parties can control the amount they invest in settlement talks and make reasonable judgments about when to try the case and when not to. Prolonged settlement conferencing can be as adverse to the client as prolonged litigation activity. See

What To Do When a Claim Strikes, a speech by Lee Novich to the Association of Engineering Firms Practicing in the Geosciences, National Meeting, April 8, 1991

9. ABA Model Rule provides:

> A lawyer shall explain a matter to the extent reasonably necessary to permit the client to make informed decisions regarding the representation

See note 3. See also Donald A. Burkhardt and Frederic K. Conover, II, "The Ethical Duty to Consider Alternatives to Litigation," *The Colorado Lawyer,* February, 1990; "Ethical Considerations in ADR," *Arbitration Journal,* March, 1990, vol. 45, no. 1 at p. 21. The Colorado Supreme Court has adopted the following addition to Rule 2.1, the state's ethics rule dealing with the lawyer's role as advisor: "In a matter involving or expected to involve litigation, a lawyer shall advise the client of alternative forms of dispute resolution which might reasonably be pursued to attempt to resolve the legal dispute, or to reach the legal objective sought." "Colorado Adopts Ethics Rule," *Alternatives to the High Cost of Litigation* (Center for Public Resources), May 1992, at 70, 71.

10. See chapter 1, note 1, Steven Brill, "Headnotes: The New Leverage." He states,

> ". . . demand for the product that most big law firms now sell, which is hours rather than solutions—is going to drop by as much as a third. In a nutshell, the forces at work [are]:
>
> 1. The movement for litigation reform that now seems unstoppable, either in the form of changes in the laws and rules governing litigation or at least by way of litigants themselves pushing for alternatives to the full-scale wars that are the grist for so much of the old leverage profit mill.
> 2. Technological advances . . .
> 3. Clients accelerated insistence that their lawyers make cost-benefit analyses in advance in order to avoid wasted effort. . .
> 4. A general cultural backlash against all the obvious waste of money and intellect now being poured into the legal product."

6.
SELECTING A MEDIATING LAWYER

The devil is an angel, too.
— Miguel de Unamuno (in *Two Mothers*)

Lawyers can and often do tip the scales toward delaying mediation. We looked at lawyers' resistance to mediation in Chapter 5. Many more lawyers speak well of mediation than actually use it. The lawyer whose main tool is litigation is like the jeweler who made jewelry with a pipe wrench. "Oh yes," the jeweler said when queried, "it looks awkward, but I use it very, very well." The typical lawyer may well be saying: "Why should I embrace a process I know little about (when it is very likely to reduce my fees substantially)? In good conscience, I must advise caution." Generally, lawyers are not taught to value prompt resolution, unless the clients teach them.[1]

A lawyer acquaintance of some 25 years experience still shakes his head, remembering that he used to think his job was to wield the tools of the legal system to win outcomes that would satisfy clients. He changed his mind the day he saw that legal remedies were too limited and the system was too costly and slow to make this kind of outcome possible. "I'm a problem-solver," he said. "At the beginning, I check my gut feeling for whether or not the matter will ultimately be negotiated. If the overwhelming odds are that it will settle, I make my strategic decisions from then on in that context." Some lawyers aren't prepared to wean themselves away from heavy reliance on the legal system. For some, the consideration is economic. Another lawyer asked, "How has this affected your practice?" "I'm busier than ever and I'm getting better results for my clients with less effort," he replied.

Knowing What To Look For

The difficulty in selecting a lawyer is knowing what to look for and being clear about what you and the lawyer each are responsible for. Many clients look for a father-figure and then proceed to hand the lawyer the power to make decisions only clients should make in the exercise of their own good judgment. This is unwise and unfair. It is you who must be satisfied. It is not enough for the lawyer to tell you that you should be satisfied. The lawyer's job is to satisfy your reasonable expectations or tell you that this cannot be done in time for you to pursue other options.

At times, lawyers exaggerate the positive side of the situation in the initial interview, perhaps to show sympathy or to get your business. When problems with the case become evident, even very good lawyers may sit on the case, doing little or nothing, for it is hard to explain to clients that their expectations are too high. This means that for many cases, the moment of truth is the courthouse steps. It is still true that delay in getting to trial still spells delay in securing a settlement.

In states where mediation is familiar to the bar, such as Washington and California, more and more the plaintiffs' lawyers are actively seeking to have cases mediated.[2] From the point of view of a lawyer on a contingent fee, the economics are compelling. Where a satisfactory result is readily achieved, some plaintiffs' lawyers will voluntarily reduce their fees below the agreed contingent fee percentage.

Responsible lawyers will give a more balanced evaluation at the beginning, including the risks. They won't play to the prospective client's sometimes frayed emotions. They will outline the steps needed to move from where things are to final resolution and the timetable for these steps. They may or may not be familiar with mediation, but when asked, they will look into it. Good lawyers will welcome questions, be willing to discuss the possibilities of mediating early, and won't mind if you take notes on what they say. Allow the lawyer to review the notes at the conclusion to assure they are accurate, and then leave a copy.

Checking Reputation

Reputation is a good place to start in evaluating a lawyer. Generally, one can check a lawyer's reputation with other lawyers. If you don't know a lawyer well enough to do this, get a friend who does to inquire for you. But keep in mind that the bias of the bar (that's what lawyers as a group are called) is an emphasis on thoroughness and scholarship over perspective and judgment.

If you have a lawyer in mind but aren't certain of his or her skill in the mediation arena, talk with a mediator or client. The public often has a very superficial view of what a lawyer is, does, and should be. But because mediation is more accessible than the legal system to the lay person, a client who has been through mediation with a lawyer may have some useful insights. Skill in mediation is different from skill in litigation.

Success in mediation depends in large part on a party's negotiation skills. The mediator usually cannot negotiate for one party without losing the trust of the other party. The mediator will protect the integrity of the process and assure that to the extent possible, each side understands the deal it is making or the options it is rejecting. This is why it is important, when lawyers are needed, to have one sophisticated in the use of mediation and equipped with good negotiation skills.

Interviewing Prospective Lawyers

It is good practice to interview two or three good prospects. Many advisors suggest steering clear of lawyers who talk about negotiating a settlement, relying on the old view that a trial orientation will bring the best result. That is unwise. More than ninety percent of civil lawsuits settle. The question is, what did you have to go through and what did you have to spend to get to that settlement. A client or lawyer with settlement on his mind

Questions For Prospective Counsel

Tell me a little about your background.	*Let the lawyer understand you are doing an interview.*
Tell me about a couple of matters like mine that you have handled.	*Check on experience. Be specific about results and method.*
How long did each one take?	*This puts your dispute in context.*
What were the fees and costs on each of these matters?	*This shows you are interested in cost considerations.*
Tell me about your experience using mediation?	*A lawyer who always finds others unwilling has little interest.*
Have you initiated any mediations?	*Is there real commitment here?*
When can I expect my situation to resolve?	*Check for settlement as well as for trial and arbitration.*
What will it cost?	*Write this down and date it. Ask it every three months.*
What are the key factors in determining when and whether we can settle?	*Look for items within your control. It isn't always someone else's call.*
What information do we need to be able to evaluate options for resolution?	*Distinguish what is needed to try the case from what is needed to settle it.*
What does the other side need in order for them to evaluate settlement options?	*This tests collaborative thinking and a problem-solving mind.*

Fig. 4 Questions for Prospective Counsel

right from the beginning is on the right track.

A lawyer whose strength is in negotiating may recommend associating a trial counsel, even before proceeding with mediation. The trial lawyer's reputation — even when she does not participate in the mediation — is a useful bargaining chip. Lawyers with a good trial record will inspire more favorable settlements at the negotiating table. At little or no cost, you get the benefit of that by the lawyer's commitment to try your case, should it prove necessary. The negotiation lawyer may conduct the mediation. Negotiation is rarely the forte of the trial lawyer, though there are exceptions.

Here are some questions to ask yourself about your lawyer. See Figure 4 for questions to ask prospective lawyers.

Q. When you've told your story, do you sense the lawyer's concern for you as a person?

A compassionate lawyer[3] can best convey your concerns to the other side. You need to keep the focus on gaining satisfaction of reasonable goals, recognizing that over-zealousness is no asset.

Q. Does the lawyer seem resourceful?

Does he offer several different approaches and strategies to secure a prompt, negotiated resolution? If so, he will be able to retrieve the situation when things get polarized, as they frequently do. Litigation often bogs down. The lawyer who can think in extrajudicial terms is going to be more useful than one who can only think about litigation activity.

Q. What does the lawyer have to say about other matters like yours?

Listen for personal experience, and a broad grasp of what is happening in the field as a whole and in cases like yours.

Q. What is this lawyer enthusiastic about?

Trial-focused lawyers often lose interest when settlement becomes a real likelihood.[4] If the lawyer enjoys playing the whole game, including developing and pursuing deft tactics to maneuver the matter to prompt resolution, that's a good sign.

Q. How does the lawyer define success?

Do his successes include negotiated resolutions or the use of mediation? Does the lawyer understand how to use mediation or does he simply try to impress on you when not to mediate? Question the experience upon which such conclusions are based.

Conclusion

The lawyer-client relationship requires attention. The best return on your investment comes from periodic phone calls or letters, to check on any developments, get advice, discuss strategy. The poorest return on the money spent on lawyers is for litigation activity.

Avoid frequent lengthy conversations and long letters, often evidence of an unhealthy infatuation with the situation. Deal with your emotional work through therapy and use the lawyer to do legal work. If you find yourself *avoiding* calling your lawyer and letting things drift, you may be in denial about some aspect of the situation. In this case, consider getting a second opinion about the quality of your representation and the reasonableness of your expectations.

Every so often, simply review the situation to check comfort level with the lawyer. There is some duplication of effort in changing lawyers, but if the relationship isn't working, the sooner you get out of it, the better. Be open, however, to the possibility that it is your own unrealistic expectations which are causing the disappointment with the lawyer.

When you interview a prospective lawyer to help you resolve your dispute through mediation, consider the questions in Figure 4. Be clear that the visit is an interview and that you will not make up your mind for at least a day or two. As you ask the questions, check your comfort level with this lawyer.

Finally, ask if this lawyer personally will be doing the work on your case, should you retain him. If not, get the lawyer who will in fact do your work to participate in the interview. The often younger, perhaps less personable lawyer who did not attract your initial interest may, indeed, be a good bet, given adequate relevant experience. It is up to you to decide.

Notes to Chapter 6

1. In 1993, the "Survey of General Counsels and Outside Counsels" by Deloitte & Touche shows the difference in corporate and outside lawyer perceptions, based on responses from the legal departments of Fortune 1,000 companies and law firm attorneys specializing in litigation. Lowered costs and savings of time were the chief motivators for using Alternative Dispute Resolution. Outside attorneys preferred arbitration and binding procedures. Extensive users and company counsels preferred mediation. Some 78% of all ADR users expected to increase their use. The figure is 98% among extensive users. *Dispute Resolution Times* (American Arbitration Assn.), Fall, 1993, pp. 1-3.

2. An article in *The Recorder,* a San Francisco newspaper for the legal community, in February, 1994, carried the headline: "ADR Forum of Choice for Harassment Claims."

3. I am speaking here of a person who transcends the hub-bub, not one who merely hates loud noises. Compassion requires comfort with oneself. In a lawyer it must merge with a high level of professional competence.

4. See Chapter 5, n. 6, LaMothe.

PART 3

Putting Principles to Work

My cat, Tink, climbs an eight-foot ladder from time to time looking for mice in my storeroom. One day the ladder had been pulled away and was leaning against a chest. The cat climbed up with great difficulty, as it was nearly vertical. She pawed the air in disbelief, looking for the missing shelf, and then swung down head over heels, step by step, as cats do. Sometimes when we think we're doing our best to resolve a matter, we, too, are bound by habit, pawing the air, looking for resolution where it cannot be found.

7.
EVALUATING MEDIATION

And we, light half-believers of our casual creeds,
Who never deeply felt, nor clearly willed . . .
Who hesitate and falter life away,
And lose tomorrow the ground won today . . .
— Matthew Arnold

The Multi-faceted Tool

The decision to mediate is a low-risk decision. It requires a small amount of time and effort and costs are modest. You will likely learn something important. The decision to mediate is also simple. The question should be, "Why not mediate?" rather than, "Why mediate?" The standard for decision may be a function of what it will cost in human as well as economic terms to continue to pursue litigation for the next six months or more, if you don't mediate. This approach aligns the burden of the argument with the probabilities of success. In this chapter, we look at some of the factors in evaluating the use of mediation.

Mediation is personal. Mediation is an integral part of a new and more personal way of handling lawsuits and other disputes. It affords more choices about ways in which a matter may be resolved.

Planning to mediate makes routine contacts with opposing parties and counsel far more valuable. Developing an effective strategy means being aware of:

- how the other side sees the case;

- what that's based on;
- who the decision-makers are on their side;
- what their interests are;
- what other interests might be brought to bear to influence their perspective; and
- what might change their perspective.

As you seek to understand the situation at these subtle levels you free your perspective of those assumptions which often turn out to be wrong. Communications automatically improve as a result of your increased attentiveness. Mediation promotes understandings difficult to achieve in unaided discussions. It helps you define and implement a strategy to head off far-ranging formal, legal investigation, the discovery which most of the time will prove unnecessary.

In early mediation, you have a chance to sell the proposition that what you are interested in is a fair and just result based on the realities of the situation. Some lawyers routinely disarm the opposing counsel by saying (and meaning), "If my client doesn't have a case, I want to know it now and we'll go away. There's no point in putting us all through a lot of work if it's going to be in vain." This can do away with a lot of game-playing in counsel communications.

Direct communications such as these don't have much impact in the stylized form of advocacy where posturing and fencing have been developed to an art form. By the values lawyers were taught, these are part of the tool kit. Without communication, negotiation is ignored until the case staggers and falls of its own weight into some kind of settlement, close to the courthouse steps.

Lawyers are like the two psychiatrists walking in opposite directions down the street. As the doctors pass, they look at one another, smile, nod. A few feet further along, each stops and half-turns, muttering, "I wonder what he meant by that?" Advocates become suspicious, too, assuming that any indication of openness by an opponent is insincere.

The truth is that the dispute is a problem to be solved, not a war to be won. Understanding this is the first step in dissolving the impasse. Most of the time, a matter can be settled on reasonable terms at almost any point along the road. By thinking adversarially, we miss myriad opportunities to reach a negotiated resolution.

Mediation is safer for making tough calls. Sometimes in litigation, a kind of camaraderie develops. This can provide an opportunity to steer the matter into mediation. For example, it might lead to an agreement by counsel for a joint discussion with a key physician in a personal injury case. Sometimes, injuries refuse to stabilize, making agreement on the extent of injury and medical needs nearly impossible (the plaintiff takes the most pessimistic view, the defendant, the most optimistic). In situations where injuries haven't yet healed and may never really settle down, the best estimate of the physician, tested in the intimacy of a private conference with both counsel, may come to be accepted by both sides, making difficult cases easier to settle.

Mediation may be used to showcase important evidence. Using mediation to enhance the impact of significant evidence and to convey that impact to the parties that need it is far more productive than planning the big bomb for that unlikely day in court.

Case example: the silver bullet. The executives and counsel for a manufacturing company reluctantly agreed to mediate, when the mediator informed them of the plaintiff's invitation. They knew the case should resolve, but they'd be damned if they would pay any significant amount on what they saw as a false claim. The day of the mediation, the plaintiff, alleging sexual harassment leading to constructive discharge and a nervous breakdown, arrived with her husband and two lawyers.

The case manager came into the mediator's office and said, "The plaintiff is here."

"How do you know?"

"There's only one person out there smoking, drinking coffee

and shaking like a leaf."

The mediator went out to personally greet the plaintiff, her husband and her lawyers. She took the plaintiff's hand in both of hers and asked, "How do you feel?"

The answer was obvious, but having the mediator visibly aware of the situation began to build rapport. As the mediator left to greet the other parties, their lawyers and claims professionals, the plaintiff handed her the remains of the cup of coffee and agreed to begin drinking water. They agreed she would use a signal if she needed a break and to try some relaxation techniques, if she found herself feeling panicky during the mediation.

The company had been defending this case for some three years, believing the plaintiff was lying. The plaintiff's counsel finally got a silver bullet — the testimony of a Ph.D. psychologist now living 2,000 miles away, who happened to be in a local bar where he observed the foreman making advances on the plaintiff in a highly sexual manner. The lawyers knew this testimony could dramatically change the other side's view of the case. Nevertheless, they sat on it for months, believing that its impact would be wasted in any kind of adversarial process except trial. They sought mediation after successfully resolving another case in mediation.

At the mediation, the plaintiff's counsel held back the silver bullet in the joint session. In the second caucus, they shared it with the mediator. Little by little, they authorized the mediator to share it in the defense caucus, which in fact maximized its impact as the afternoon progressed. It was not easy for the defense, its insurance carriers and counsel to change a view they had held so firmly and so long. But they found this new evidence compelling.

Using the caucusing process to present the evidence gave the defense team time before they had to respond. They also had an opportunity to evaluate the evidence with their own investigator whose earlier call to this witness triggered his memory. Having all these interests present at the mediation saved months of negotiating who would contribute, and how much, toward an overall settlement. The defense revised its estimate of the value of the case and the case settled at the end of the day with what is called a structure, a long-term payout much like an annuity, which can have periodic and lump sum payments. This satisfied the plaintiff and reflected a mutually satisfactory value of the claim.

Timing Considerations

The appropriate timing of mediation depends in part on what kind of mediation you use. This is discussed in Chapter 8, *Selecting a Mediator.* In traditional mediations, it is safe to use the procedure at any time, since any mediator reactions adverse to your side will be shared with you confidentially in private caucus during the mediation. It is useful to have this opportunity to test your theories of the case on this disinterested party fairly early in the process, whether on not you settle.[1]

Circumstances also may offer you opportunities to play off scheduled court or discovery activity, to give added incentive to settle. Reaching agreement in mediation, for example, might avoid some impending unpleasant or risky event, such as a party's deposition or the hearing on a motion for summary judgment. Such deadlines are not necessary, however, to make mediation effective. The mediator's skill builds commitment to the joint endeavor to reach agreement.

Mediation works late. The most widely-used timing for mediation is days or weeks before trial, an endgame strategy. This is the easiest time to get counsel to agree to mediate. It is encouraged by court programs addressed primarily to meeting the courts' needs for fewer cases requiring trials rather than the parties' needs for cost-effective resolution. Endgame mediations do resolve cases but the majority of benefits which mediation could secure are lost.

Early mediation works better. Early mediation offers an opportunity to capitalize on whatever flexibility remains with parties, before they become polarized by litigation activities. It can significantly lower the transaction costs for cases that are frivolous and not worth the effort to defend. It is also often used in cases where the litigation costs border on astronomical, such as toxic torts, wrongful termination and construction cases. By approaching early mediation with an open mind, preparation costs can be saved, pending an assessment of what, really, is needed.[2] Cases frequently settle in early mediation, because it turns out nothing more is needed.

One product of early mediation is the *procedural agreement.* These agreements describe what the parties will do and when they will do it, to secure the information they need to reach final agreement. In a subsequent mediation or through subsequent mediator telephone follow-up, the case usually settles.

Here are some examples of the way people have used early mediation.

· *Investigatory Mediation.* Regardless of the stage of discovery, mediation allows balanced and candid exploration of the perceptions of witnesses. Witnesses may be gradually offered on both sides as questions arise during the mediation. The mediator conducts the questioning in person or by speaker phone. This procedure may narrow differences sufficiently that parties can negotiate.

· *Mediated Discovery.* With or without counsel, experts and principals may have a detailed discussion of the information each party becomes willing to give concerning a key issue. The mediator keeps information-giving in balance, records progress, isolates hot issues and identifies areas of agreement. This may generate statements of agreement and disagreement, and show where more information is needed. The parties may negotiate a plan for addressing essential concerns. This type of mediation narrows the dispute so that settlement discussions can be productive and saves months to years of formal discovery effort.[3]

· *Pre-termination Mediation.* When an employment relationship is in trouble, mediation enables those involved to discuss the situation and develop options in the face of likely termination followed by a complaint. It may involve counsel for the employee, otherwise in the background. It diffuses the emotional charge implicit in the situation.

· *Keeping the Job Going.* When a construction project is faltering, early mediation among principals often affords perspective on responsibility and creativity in devising needed fixes. Usually, it enables the job to carry on.

· *Joint Inspection.* When physical circumstances are significant, mediation has produced an agreement for joint inspection of sites, sometimes including the mediator, where a prompt return to mediation and further negotiation is planned.

Even with mediations on the courthouse steps, information critical to the parties' evaluation of options for resolution is often missing. With few exceptions, litigation usually fails to get the information needed to evaluate settlement options until the often bitter end. It is a myth that you need to wait until all discovery is complete to use mediation effectively. And when you know almost everything about the case, mediation helps you focus on what's critical in all of that information.

Questions and Answers

What is mediable? Almost anything is mediable. You can profitably mediate anything requiring a decision by two or more people. Mediation has been introduced into the school ground, where trained youngsters use a form of it to help their classmates resolve differences. Remember when you were a teenager and you wanted to use the family car on Friday night?[4] Dad might have said something like, "Hell, no. The last time you used the car it had so little gas in the tank, I couldn't even back out of the garage. Did you think it was some kind of calf so you could wean it?"

Mom may have mediated, or rather, conciliated the discussion: "Perhaps you two could agree on how much gas would have to be left in the tank." Mom was a conciliator because she had an interest in the outcome.[5] She wanted peace. A mediator, technically, has no interest in the outcome. It is the parties' business to decide whether the outcome will be war or peace or something in between.

Some examples of mediable disputes appear in figure 5.

When is it unwise to mediate? The decision to mediate must be made in the context of other options, including litigation. Is litigation a preferable forum? How costly is delay? Is there a business relationship to preserve or restore? If litigation proceeds full-bore, how will costs balance against both possible and probable returns?[6]

Court resolution may be needed for political reasons. For example, some issues are so controversial that at least one side does not want to take responsibility for voluntarily participating in its resolution. Examples include the school desegregation cases and high-stakes corporate disputes.

A truly non-mediable situation is one where the other party is absent. Certainly, you cannot mediate with an absent party, unless you can find an authorized representative (what small businesses desperately need when something goes wrong with an offshore contract). Litigating is relatively more attractive in this situation since you can take a default judgment and try to find some assets from which to collect it.

Myths about what is not mediable. In the early days of mediation, much was written about what was not mediable. Today, some lawyers still have doubts about the process.[7] But experience has taught us most disputes *are* mediable. Many matters characterized as non-mediable have done very well in mediation. Also, the alternatives to mediating are sometimes so poor, mediation becomes desirable by comparison.

One example is mediating with someone who is marginally competent. While this may not be attractive, it may be better than litigating with such a person. Hard as it is, the marginally competent are better to deal with in mediation than in the courts. In mediation, they may have representatives and advisers and family members involved. There need be no time pressure, so that they have the fairest, most complete opportunity to evaluate their options and decide what to do. The mediator is there to be sure

EXAMPLES OF MEDIABLE DISPUTES

Debtors and Creditors

- collection claims
- bankruptcy matters
- foreclosures
- lender liability

Business Relationships

- real estate
- employment and work place
- construction disputes
- copyright/trademark
- insurance coverage disputes
- franchise agreements
- professional liability
- product liability
- almost all contract disputes
- trade secrets
- landlord/tenant
- licensing agreements
- intra-organizational disputes
- partnership disputes

Personal Relationships

- marriage and divorce
- elder care disputes
- probate battles among heirs
- child custody
- family business disputes
- neighbor disputes

The Larger World

- toxic cleanup issues
- disputes over disasters
- resource management
- international trade issues
- matters pending in arbitration
- personal injury suits
- resource allocation fights
- solid waste siting
- matters pending in litigation
- property damage disputes

Fig. 5 Types of mediable disputes

their concerns are heard and understood and that they understand what their options are.

The rule governing mediator practice in a case of marginal

competency is that a mediator must terminate a mediation if the parties are not competent to negotiate. In questionable situations, the presence of counsel may make it possible to continue, although the lawyer then has the problem of deciding to what extent the client is "there." For example, in one Arizona mediation over a coach's long-term sexual harassment of one member of his college women's swimming team, the plaintiff was extremely fragile.

Her counsel, working closely with her therapist, did an excellent job of piloting her through two days of mediation, in an effort to settle the case. The plaintiff, however, could not stick to any decision about what relief would be acceptable. This made it clear that trial, hard as it would be for such a fragile person, was the only alternative.

The matter eventually was tried and the plaintiff won a large verdict, only to be reduced substantially, later, in the court's discretion.

Another reason often given for not mediating is that one party wants to delay a decision for as long as possible, as for example, in collection matters. Parties using litigation to delay could as easily use their *ability* to delay as a bargaining chip in a negotiation where it might be traded for something of value impossible to get in litigation.

Another example of a situation thought inappropriate for mediation is a matter in which you want to set a legal precedent. It is true that mediation cannot set a legal precedent. But precedent-setting is always a gamble. In *Borel vs. Fibreboard*, the company, seeking to set a legal precedent, appealed a Texas jury's award of $80,000 to the widow of an asbestos worker in a wrongful death action. But the 5th Circuit *affirmed* the award, writing a landmark decision applying strict liability to asbestos (thereby igniting the asbestos litigation explosion). Given the risks, mediated discussions are worth considering.

Not infrequently, the precedent-oriented party decides this is not the right case to try to establish the precedent and the alternatives to judicial resolution are attractive enough for the matter to settle. There are many opportunities for derailment of principle-oriented litigation, which also may afford opportunities to resolve through mediation. At times, enforceability can be secured through a mediated stipulated order or judgment.

Would you want to mediate a matter when you simply want a declaration that you're right? You might say, "Absolutely not," but this response misses the point. Yes, you may win at trial. But wouldn't you rather win at the table, where you have complete control over the outcome? If you don't mediate, you'll never know what your alternatives to trial really are. Defendants who are "clean" — without blame — and who *look* clean can and do walk away scot-free in mediation, particularly in multi-party mediations. Plaintiffs often prefer certainty of outcome when given a chance to consider all the options.

Some have used as an example of nonmediability the situation where one wants to clear his wrongfully tarnished name. In truth, a quietly mediated agreement to secure favorable counter-publicity might do a great deal more for one's reputation than media reports repeatedly raising the malignant accusation before the public while the libel or slander litigation is pending.

Would a party bent on "rolling the dice" want to mediate? They might, as plaintiffs, hit the jackpot or as defendants win a defense verdict. Such people assume they will get less by mediating than by trying their case. While this may be true in some cases, it is not true across the board. Defendants have refused to pay what turned out to be a fraction of what a jury assessed against them. Some plaintiffs have turned down more in mediation than they eventually recovered at trial. They also lost the chance to structure the settlement in financially-advantageous ways.

Many insist mediation is not an option because of the other side's unwillingness. The barrier is often not the other side's unwillingness, but the *belief.* It is so common a misperception that the rule of thumb should be to ignore it. If you have not been able to get the other side to agree to mediation, use a convener. Parties learn to want to mediate through the patience and skills of the convener. (See Chapter 9, *Preparing for Mediation,* "Convening.")

Turning a "no" into a "I'll give it a try," is challenging and productive work. Tactically, the focus is on never letting a "no" become final, by working with the interests of the reluctant party.

For a long time, it was thought you could not mediate matters in which a serious crime was involved. But the criminal justice system offers little to victims. Victim-offender mediations began, according to the *Wall Street Journal*, in Canada in 1977, with the help of the Mennonites. Research by Professor Mark S. Umbreit, professor of social work at University of Minnesota, shows that victim-perpetrator restitution mediations are productive in many ways. The victims lose some of their fear. Perpetrator recidivism goes down and restitution is made much more often.[8]

If there ever was a need for a protective arena for the discussion of terribly painful events, it is in cases of rape, incest, robbery and murder. Convicted perpetrators can sometimes realize the depth of the pain and grief they have inflicted. Victims can let go of the victim-stance and move on with their lives. Restitution mediations are very delicate and each side needs their support in place, either present or just outside the mediation. There may need to be a pre-mediation evaluation of the parties to assure suitability as well as screening to assure that the mediator or mediators are compassionate, highly skilled and experienced in such matters.

One lawyer well-versed in mediation recommends mediating if you know enough to negotiate — I would add, if you know what you would like to negotiate for — and if both sides have a good faith interest in the discussion.[9] Some observers worry about mediating prematurely, as it might be unnecessary.[10] I consider it a low-cost insurance policy protecting against the far greater wasted litigation expense.

Considerations such as the cost must be weighed against what you will accomplish with the same money if you don't mediate. What will likely happen if you don't mediate now? Is an eighty percent chance of success good enough?

How final is mediation? Finality is a buzzword in dispute resolution. As a practical matter, a mediated resolution has a quality of finality unapproachable in adjudicated disputes. The dispute receives a decent burial and the resulting agreement is non-appealable. (One would have to file a whole new lawsuit to attack it.) The parties have invested both time and effort in reaching this agreement. They reached it voluntarily, believing it served their best interests.[11] There are times in any mediation when finality through court action may need to be added, to provide for enforcement of the private agreement. At times, for example, parties decide to make their mediated agreement the heart of a stipulated judgment in the pending action, so that judicial enforcement is available.

Another way of assuring finality is to have the mediator, *after a mediated agreement is reached,* become an arbitrator for the purposes of making the agreement an arbitration award. This is probably the ultimate finality, as there is little that can upset an arbitration award.

Court judgments may make one or both sides feel they weren't even heard. Mediation lets them know they were heard and that they controlled the outcome. This leaves little reason to attack the agreement of settlement.

If no agreement is reached, mediation is a milestone along the way, producing other desirable outcomes, such as lowering hostilities, clarifying focus and learning what needs to be done to resolve.

What are the preconditions to mediation? The only preconditions to mediation are those needed for any negotiation. Does the other side know they have to deal with you? Do you have their attention? Do they know that your claim or defense has substance?

Substance is established automatically in most cases, because the existence of a viable claim or defense is obvious. Even in situations where the weight of your position comes from procedural advantage (your ability to require or delay action by the other side), there can still be enough substance on your side to win agreement to mediate.

When the theories of recovery (the legal underpinnings of claims) are new, when liability is slim and damages heavy, a prospective defendant may not believe he has to deal with you. Often, in addition, a party may be misinformed. Based on what they have been told, they may see no merit to the claim or defense. Mediation usually exposes these errors and tests the plausibility of difficult theories, once you can get the other side to the table.

When someone isn't listening to you, you can still offer to listen to them.[12] "You seem pretty convinced of your position. Let's spend a few hours in mediation and see what we can accomplish. Maybe there's something we've overlooked." It is easy to hear this statement as an admission that *you* have overlooked something, rather than that *both* may have overlooked something. No matter. The object is to get an opportunity for serious discussions and this will often accomplish the purpose.

Does it make sense to mediate a frivolous case? When you believe there is little substance to a claim or defense, should you mediate anyway? In mediation, you can check on what they've got. You may be missing something or they may be. In mediation, you may test your assumptions; if you're still convinced there is no merit on the other side, impress them with your determination to resist or persist. *Agreeing to mediate does not mean agreeing to resolve.*

Is it necessary to litigate first to get the other side's attention? Lawyers often use litigation activity to impress opposing counsel with the need to give a claim or defense serious attention. In large cases, after perhaps a year and a half on the discovery rock pile, when tens of thousands of pages of documents are produced and copied and indexed, you have the other side's attention. This is often gross overkill.

A lawyer with a great trial record automatically commands the opposing party's attention. Some lawyers' names on the file may have the opposite effect. Clients simply need to be alert to the situation. Today the tactic of hindering and delaying just claims has risen to an art form, which makes litigation far riskier and mediation far more compelling.

Filing a lawsuit usually gets someone's attention, but at considerable price, particularly if there are allegations the defendant will see as insulting. In mediation, at least you can find out where the problem lies. Is it counsel or client? If client, who? And why? All of this information will be useful in designing your long-range strategy.

How trustworthy is information secured through mediation? Information made available through mediation can have the same marks of trustworthiness as that elicited through formal discovery. For example, it can be submitted with a declaration as to its nature and extent under penalty of perjury. That simply needs to be an item for negotiation. Fisher and Ury point out in *Getting To Yes* that in a negotiation, it is unwise to trust the other side. This is sound advice. Meaningful trust builds gradually from experience. You will learn to recognize how far to trust, if you do not already know. Ultimately, trust is essential. But it must be earned. We earn trust ourselves by being reliable and by giving our attention to the other side's concerns.

What does mediation cost? Overall, the cost of using mediation is about ten percent or less of the cost of relying exclusively on litigation. Some community dispute resolution programs and some court programs still provide free mediation. For private mediations, the cost is often split at least two ways and is usually less than the cost of a deposition. In round numbers, it might cost you from $300 (for a small claims or support payment mediation) to $3,000 (for complex or sensitive commercial mediation) per day of mediation. In rare, high stakes mediations, certain mediators, perhaps those whose connections are essential to resolution, might charge as much as $25,000 per day. The cost is meaningful only in comparison to what your alternatives are. It may make sense to pay $1,500 for a day of mediation if you would otherwise spend $150,000, or even $15,000, on litigation before the year is out.

Some mediators work by the hour, some by the day. Some charge higher fees for more sensitive and complex matters, and lesser fees for smaller cases, to remain competitive. Contingent fees, those based on the outcome, are not available, to my knowledge; the mediator needs to be free to allow the parties to fail to reach agreement. Occasionally, where the parties' tempers are frayed and just getting started is nearly impossible, mediators will allow the parties to pay what they think the service is worth, after the mediation. At times, even in commercial cases, the parties will mediate the division of the fee.

What about fee-sharing? Compared to litigation, the cost of mediation is very small. Sometimes parties get upset about who pays what part of the cost. There is a value in having all parties contribute, but no particular advantage in having the contribution be equal. The mediator *must* be neutral, to be of any use. Unlike an arbitrator, the mediator makes no decision. Everything he does happens in plain view of one or both parties. Equal sharing is important only if a party thinks it is.

How long do mediations last? Most civil lawsuits are resolved in mediation in a few hours to a day. Particularly complex disputes such as business contract disputes and some construction disputes may go two days. Generally, even a complex mediation is unlikely to last more than a few days, although there are situations where mediation is used to facilitate technical discussions in which the mediation can go on for weeks.[14] In these situations, litigation is very likely to go on for years. In public policy and environmental matters not in litigation, the mediations are still measured in days, but they often occur over months. In such matters, preparation time is key and so the number of mediation days is relatively few.

What is the level of principal participation in mediation? In some mediations such as divorce, only the principals are present, as a rule. In business mediations, client and counsel work together as a team during the mediation. Sometimes, the client just listens, saving comments for private meetings with counsel, with or without the mediator present. Sometimes, the principal is an active if not leading participant. This is a strategic decision based on maximizing the benefits of mediating.

Does mediation satisfy the need for one's day in court? In good mediations, participants, regardless of their level of active participation, tend to view the experience as having their day in court. Their side is presented. Their counsel is at their side and visibly *on* their side. The bad news — the downside — is delivered by the mediator whose perspective they can evaluate for themselves. There is often more complete examination of disputes in mediation than in trial, due to rules of evidence and greater formality.

Conclusion

The decision to mediate is only as big as we need it to be. Mediation is simple and straightforward. Why not mediate? There is little to lose and much to gain. If no settlement is reached, the parties can often agree on what is needed so the *next* meeting will make resolution possible. The process of resolution has begun.

Mediation literally turbo-charges negotiations. Why does this happen? It happens because the parties drop the defensive, adversarial, distrustful stance they took on as part of litigation and become more the problem-solving, justice-seeking, compassionate human beings they have been all along.

Notes to Chapter 7

1. You can learn about your hurdles by engaging a mediator to give a reaction to your side of the case even without benefit of a mediation. Mediators serve as settlements experts, whose job it is to look for weaknesses in a side's position with possibly overlooked options for resolution. They are often expert negotiation strategists, as well.

2. See Chapter 5, note 8, Novich, *What To Do When a Claim Strikes.*

3. See John Forester, "Planning in the Face of Conflict: Mediated Negotiation Strategies in Practice," Chapter 6 in *Planning in the Face of Power,* (1990) pp. 82-106, for a comparable model of mediating land use planning issues; See also *Using Joint Fact-Finding Techniques to Resolve Complex Environmental Policy Disputes,* CONCUR working paper 92-02, Scott T. McCreary, John K Gamman and Cornelia Tietke, 1992, for a similar approach in that arena.

4. This story is drawn, in part, from the training work of William F. Lincoln, of National Center Associates in Tacoma, Wash., my first mediation teacher and mentor.

5. Frequently, the terms "mediator" and "conciliator" are used interchangeably. I find it more useful to make the distinction between one disinterested in the outcome (a mediator) and one who has an interest in the outcome (a conciliator). The Federal Mediation and Conciliation Service, for example, is mandated to help keep industrial peace. By this definition, their mediators would be considered conciliators.

6. For a thoughtful discussion, see n. 4, Chapter 1, Singer, pp. 82-83.

7. Several examples are found in Peter Lovenheim's useful book, *Mediate, Don't Litigate* (McGraw-Hill Publishing Co.), 1989, pp. 26-29. See Chapter 5, n .5, LaMothe, "Opening Statement: Thinking About Mediation," for example, listing as not appropriate for mediation situations where dispositive motions might end the case. The pendency of such motions is a useful bargaining chip in many mediations and courts are reluctant to grant such motions..

8. "Victim-Perpetrator Reconciliations Grow in Popularity," Ellen Joan Pollock, *Wall Street Journal,* October 28, 1993.

9. Wulff, "A Mediation Primer," *Donovan, Leisure, Newton & Irvine ADR Practice Book,* pp. 113-136 (John H. Wilkinson, ed.), 1990.

10. See the comprehensive treatise by Nancy Rogers and Craig

McEwen, *Mediation, Law, Policy and Practice,* Clark, Boardman, Callahan, 1989, p. 26.

11. Compulsory mediation seriously interferes with the qualities of voluntary mediation that tend toward finality. So does the use of coercion in mediation, for example, when court-appointed mediators makes recommendations to the judge.

12. This is in accordance with the mechanical view of human communication: "To open ears, operate mouth."

13. These estimates of duration assume traditional mediation is being used. If you are using advisory mediation, it can go much shorter (an hour or two instead of three or four) or much longer (two weeks rather than two or three days). I believe these differences are inherent in the nature of the processes.

    Advisory mediation can be shorter when the facts are simple and known, since the advisor's focus is on giving his opinion. Traditional mediators will take the safer tack of building the parties' awareness of where justice lies, without giving advice.

    In complex matters, the traditional mediator's expertise in what is not essential saves a great deal of time. The advisory mediator is burdened with the responsibility of giving sound advice and therefore labors much harder to be sure all arguments are heard and understood.

8.
SELECTING A MEDIATOR

Education consists mainly in
what we have unlearned. — Mark Twain

Unlike litigation, which resembles the trial-by-combat that it replaced, mediation has a quality of intimacy. The choice of mediator is a delicate decision with many consequences. A mediator is one who helps the parties reach their own resolution, although the term "mediator" has been used, loosely, to include advice-givers and even decision-makers.[1] In selecting a mediator, it is useful to bear in mind the counsel of ADR pioneer Lon Fuller:

> The central quality of mediation [is] its capacity to reorient the parties towards each other, not by imposing rules on them, but by helping them to achieve a new and shared perception of their relationship [and the situation], a perception that will redirect their attitude and dispositions toward one another.[2]

This quality is just as important in a personal injury mediation as it is in a partnership mediation.

What Does A Mediator Do?

One of the most overlooked services of the mediator is convening the parties. The mediator, mediation firm or mediation case manager is there to entice the opposing party to the table for you.

The better conveners will succeed in this more than eighty percent of the time.[3] You do not need to have an agreement to mediate in order to file a matter in mediation. Some of the techniques used by professionals to convene a mediation are set forth in Chapter 9, *Preparing to Mediate*.

A second often-ignored function of the mediator is to focus the parties in their preparation, either jointly or in separate caucuses, as they may agree. This subject is discussed in Chapter 9, in the section titled, "Strategic Preparation."

The focus of this chapter, however, is on what the mediator does in the mediation itself. Mediation, despite its ancient antecedents in tribal cultures, is still in its infancy as a modern approach to dispute resolution. To date, it has afforded little insight into its subtle and powerful process. Yet of necessity, court-annexed mediation programs, community dispute programs and many others have for years recruited and trained people to be mediators without a clear understanding of mediation's requirements and promise.

Christopher Honeyman and the Wisconsin Employment Relations Commission began in 1985 to develop criteria for evaluating mediators and began working to devise tests to check performance against them.[4] Not long thereafter, the Massachusetts Office of Dispute Resolution worked with Honeyman's criteria, in a court-annexed mediation program for a court of general jurisdiction, made some modifications and found them useful in developing a quality mediation program.[5] At about the same time, the Society of Professionals in Dispute Resolution (SPIDR) established a Commission on Qualifications. Its 1989 report concluded that in general, the market place could be sufficiently discriminatory as to quality. But with mandatory programs and those in which the parties have no effective means to influence the selection of mediators, the report suggested that standards should be set to ensure consistency and quality in the delivery of services.[6] Then in 1993, a group called the Test Design Project, chaired by Honeyman developed a set of *Interim Guidelines for Selecting Mediators*. which was published by the National Institute for Dispute Resolution (NIDR).[7]

The problem with the concept of marketplace screening is that in most states the marketplace is ill-informed about mediation. It is only after experiencing a variety of mediators and mediation styles that the ability to discriminate develops. Several years ago, a lawyer told me that a well-known mediator had "mediated on him" two years earlier. "My arm still hurts from the experience," he said. Attila the Mediator[8] is often far less skillful than his quieter sisters and brothers and may use dominance to define the outcome rather than making it possible for the parties to design their own. One of the fundamental shared views among experienced mediators is that self-determination — voluntary and uncoerced agreements made by parties free to leave at any time — is a critical quality of mediation.[9]

In one situation, a mediator was criticized in a *Wall Street Journal* article for allowing the parties in a farm-credit dispute to get into a shouting match. The lender's representative, however, conceded he ended up with a reasonable settlement.[10] Was it because the farmer could at last vent his feelings or in spite of it? There is nothing about a shouting match in itself that indicates the mediator isn't competent. In fact, one indicator of mediator competence is the ability to allow the honest expression of feelings, while keeping discussions on track through virtually transparent controls.

From the sometimes heated debate over professional standards, several themes emerge. First, the findings from Wisconsin and Massachusetts concur with the Commission on Qualifications of the Society of Professionals in Dispute Resolution (SPIDR)[11] in a surprising conclusion: no particular type or degree of prior education or job experience is an effective predictor of success as a mediator (or arbitrator, for that matter). This means that mediators are best selected and evaluated on their performance by their clients and professional observers. With an understanding of what mediators do and how mediation works, you will be far more successful in finding the mediator who will do the best job.

The work of Honeyman, the Project and its critics is exciting to the mediation community. For years mediation has been considered so personal — an art, not a science — that it defied analysis. Honeyman and his successors are proving otherwise. They found that while styles differed widely, good mediators had several things in common. From these efforts, I have culled a list which to me seems most useful for our purposes.

• *Information gathering.*[12] Good mediators engage in intensive factual inquiry early in the case. It may be general or highly focused on what the parties and mediator see as the critical facts, for purposes of the discussion. It may be done in joint session or in private caucus or both. This is the foundation for everything that follows. The mediator's effectiveness in devil's advocacy — showing you the weaknesses of your position — depends on being seen as knowledgeable about the dispute. An important multi-faceted mediator tool for investigating is the "readback,"[13] discussed in Chapter 10, *The Art of Mediating,* "Quality of Space."

• *Empathy.* Good mediators win your trust by being willing to hear and discuss what concerns you, whether or not it is strictly relevant to the dispute. They understand the situation from your perspective and let you know that. Their ability to sift what's important from what is said, to pare down overstated positions by "reframing," and their appropriate sense of humor gradually wins your belief in their competence.

• *Impartiality.* "Impartiality" means not favoring a particular result, while "neutrality" means not favoring a particular party.[14] In mediators, a lack of trustworthiness can literally spoil the process. *Mediators must be neutral, or they are of no use to anyone.* As one lawyer said after a successful mediation, "I thought I wanted a mediator who was favorable to our side. I learned that I needed one who was favorable to all sides. If I had gotten my wish, the other side would never have trusted enough for us to be able to negotiate this settlement."

• *Persuasion.* Often, mediators take steps early to obtain small concessions. This builds a pattern of agreements which helps you believe the discussions will be fruitful — to suspend your disbelief for the period of the mediation. This is subtle persuasion, not argument for a position or outcome. As the mediation progresses, the mediator's intensity increases, creating a sense of urgency about getting the matter resolved now. Some people think only loud or controlling neutrals are persuasive. Experience suggests the opposite is true. You often make the quiet mediator's voice your own, persuading yourself.

• *Generating options.*[15] A mediator cannot contribute much to devising options for resolution until the parties believe she is knowledgeable about the situation. Early attempts, however brilliant, are seen as condescending and can prevent the parties from reaching their own agreement. Good mediators are not ego-invested in their suggestions or proposals, allowing you to use them or not. They are, however, creative and not afraid to repackage ideas that were passed over previously. They are also a source of ideas about how to overcome significant hurdles.

• *Distraction.* Mediation is hard work. You are called on to challenge your assumptions and recognize your fantasies about how the matter may resolve. You labor over your side of the negotiation process. Good mediators provide distractions to ease the tension.

There are two other skills identified in the Massachusetts Program. Both describe aspects of maintaining the focus and flow of the mediation process.

• *Managing the interaction.* This includes maintaining appropriate control over the process. Some mediators are experts at keeping counsel and parties at the task, creative and productive, without seeming to exert pressure. They prevent bullying and create space for a *party* to speak, an opportunity that can get lost, when lawyers are involved. They respond constructively to pressure tactics, including personal attacks, for in part their role is one of lightning rod. Distraction helps in this. They establish early agreement about what the objective of the meeting is and what, if any, rules will govern the parties during the mediation. Rules might include speaking in turn or not talking abusively of or to anyone.

• *Strategic direction.* It is one thing to juggle a lot of balls. It is another to give that activity direction, purpose and meaning. With this skill, the mediator works with the parties' real agendas, their underlying interests and the pivotal issues needing exploration in order to keep the parties' efforts productive. Without it, mediation can bog down.

Mediator Qualifications and Skills

In addition to these skills,[16] a good mediator works under several professional and ethical constraints which are important to us. The first injunction is to do no harm.[17] Many beginners use techniques that work sometimes, but carry a significant risk of prejudice to the negotiations when they don't work. Proposing one's own idea as such to one side, without having a very good sense that it would be acceptable to the other side, is an example.[18]

A second rule of good mediation practice is never to attempt to work beyond the parties' trust level. Trust ebbs and flows during a mediation. It is often lowest when the mediator says something you don't want to hear. You feel pressured and disrespected when a mediator ignores your distrust. Good mediators stop. They come back and work to rebuild trust, so that the arena for collaborative problem-solving is big enough to get a good result.

It is obvious that to be good, a mediator must be highly skilled and must possess some special personal traits. Among those identified in the Interim Guidelines are sensitivity, emotional stability, integrity, maturity (not just age), impartiality and insight into themselves and their clients.

Other abilities desirable in a mediator are reasoning, analyzing, problem-solving, reading comprehension, writing (sometimes mediators draft agreements at the conclusion of mediations) and oral and non-verbal communication skills. Finally, above all, is commitment: you want a mediator who will not give up easily. Tenacity is a big part of mediator effectiveness.

The work of the Test Design Project, the Massachusetts program and the many critics and commentators drawn into the discussion are demystifying mediation in a significant breakthrough. Many in the mediation field are reluctant to see so-called objective testing (such as most state bar examinations) used for a performance-oriented profession like mediation. Such tests by their nature examine only the ability to recall information the candidates have memorized, not their ability to mediate. Many also are passionately committed to "letting many flowers bloom," by avoiding setting up one model of mediation as the standard against which all are measured, thereby stifling the innovation and creativity which are such an important part of mediation today. Performance testing,[19] particularly if combined with some kind of peer review process, is most promising.

The Interim Guidelines were developed in an atmosphere of increasing legislative interest in the certification of mediators.[20] Most professionals are certified by some authority. Why not mediators? In these discussions, it is easy to forget the burdens that a wider awareness imposes upon the definition of a profession. Today, we are acutely aware of the sexual, ethnic, racial and cultural biases that sneak into the establishment of norms. Professions depend for their existence on exclusivity, often hard to square with these important considerations. A critical conclusion of the SPIDR Report and the Interim Guidelines, recognizing these needs is that, "No single entity (rather, a variety of organizations) should establish qualifications for neutrals."[21]

We are just getting a toehold on the concept of mediator competence. If we rush to certification or legislation on the subject, we are likely to set harmful limitations on the evolution of the profession. Mediation, like teaching, is a good field in which to move beyond paper and pencil tests of mental abilities and strive to identify professional excellence. But our conclusions will need to be tentative for some time to come.[22]

Mediator experience. A mediator's track record tells you far more than paper qualifications. A long resume of experience in other work — for example law, engineering or accounting — speaks volumes of the missing mediation experience. Here as elsewhere, objective criteria have their limitations. As your experience with mediation grows, so will your ability to find precisely the type of mediator you want for any given case.

There is no "best" mediator. In the realm of professional qualifications, it becomes obvious that different mediators are better in different areas.

When you want the mediator to be an expert in the mediation process, look for a traditional mediator. You want the mediator's reactions in confidential caucus, but you want it to be more informative than advice-giving. You want someone who finds agreements in the cacophony of the dispute when no one else can. You want someone who can hold the center when chaos threatens.

Substantive knowledge. A mediator must have sufficient knowledge of the subject matter to allow him or her to work effectively in it. For individuals who are quick studies, that may be very little — for example, a conversation with a mediator experienced in that area or an expert in the field to develop a vocabulary and a context for the particular dispute. For others, it may require years of work in the subject area. There is an advantage to having a mediator whose mind is still open on the subject, a problem at times for those with a career investment as an expert in the subject area. This is one of the characteristics you may want to evaluate in the mediator you are considering.

Some mediation services, however, provide mediators selected for their subject area expertise. If you have an agricultural dispute, they will assign a lawyer or other expert practicing in that area, rather than an expert mediator with experience in that field.[23] Among mediation services are two influential organizations, the American Arbitration Association (AAA) and the Center for Public Resources (CPR).[24] Both have contributed significantly to the education of lawyers and the consuming public about mediation. Both organizations pay attention to quality issues and are aware of the public's increasing ability to discriminate between mediators. Both now are beginning to put traditional mediators on their panels, presumably because of their effectiveness.

CPR's policy also has been to get *lawyers* to serve as mediators, as a part of their law practice. Lawyers can and do excel as mediators. However, not one of the studies we've discussed show that being a lawyer is a predictor of success as a mediator. In fact, in the Massachusetts program where mediators handled cases valued in excess of $25,000, researchers found that ". . . lawyers did not perform better than non-lawyers." The mediators needed only to be comfortable working with lawyers and the law, the study concluded.[25]

Types of Mediation: Advisory and Traditional

Advisory mediation,[26] the name given to mediations by subject-area (not necessarily mediation) experts, is evaluative in nature. Its purpose is to get a fix on the merits, sometimes of some technical issue, should the matter actually be tried. Evidentiary and technical arguments can be evaluated in this setting better than people problems.

In the hands of an experienced trial lawyer or jurist, advisory mediation also provides information about the disposition of local judges and juries. If the best way to resolve the dispute is to get an independent opinion, you may want an advisory mediation. If crafting remedies, putting people in touch with their own best judgment or dealing with difficult people is the goal, traditional mediation is more productive.

In the typical time-limited, court-type settlement conference, the neutral informs the parties of his expectations of the outcome at trial and may well tell them what he believes the case is worth. This approach requires the parties to have their information reasonably well in hand so that this advice will have meaning.

Court settlement panels are not unlike advisory mediations. These often consist of a judge, a plaintiff's lawyer and a defense lawyer who hear brief presentations by the lawyers and then place a value on the case. Sometimes it is very helpful. Sometimes, however, these panels do not give an objective opinion, hoping to influence the parties to settle. Their hearings are often too short and there may be a long wait until one's case is called.

Mediators with an apparent "bias" include lawyers specializing in work for just one side, such as defense or plaintiff work. They have particular value in certain kinds of mediation. For example, the California State Automobile Association, a company that sees many doubtful claims, uses lawyers who usually represent plaintiffs as mediators. When one of these lawyers says a plaintiff's case is weak, the plaintiff's lawyers are likely to listen.

Traditional mediation is generally free of advice. Traditional mediators usually have significant experience *mediating* the type of dispute in question, unlike advisory mediators whose expertise usually comes from practicing law or some other profession (engineering, for example) in the subject area of the dispute.

The essential expertise in traditional mediation is in mediating. If particular technical expertise is required, the mediator will often suggest bringing in a neutral expert or will bring in a technical co-mediator at the point where this is needed. It is helpful if this expert has mediation training and skill. The preference of many lawyers for "muscle mediation," something many professionals deny is mediating at all, frustrates many mediators. They may take comfort in the history of the evolution of the profession of surgeon from that of barber.[27]

Traditional mediation requires greater skill and more experience than advisory mediation. I believe there is a trend for advisory mediators to become traditional mediators, as their skill and experience grow. Traditional mediators are often experts at dealing with interpersonal problems. They may mediate in one field only, such as family law, where they develop intimate familiarity with the problems of the field, or they may be generalists. Generalists offer opportunities for cross-fertilization, bringing to the situation techniques and strategies used in other types of disputes.

Functional Differences In Types of Mediation

Early intervention. Traditional mediation is useful at any stage. In matters too early to settle, parties seek agreement on what is needed and how to get it, so that both sides may evaluate settlement options. One doesn't have to write 10 letters or make 20 telephone calls to get what is needed. Moreover, less preparation is required because there is more control in a traditional mediation. Settlement efforts may be halted at any time and the agenda turned to what each side needs to know to be able to resolve, and how to get it.

The need to know. This is greatest in fact-finding processes, somewhat less in advisory mediations and much less in traditional mediations. This is important in a universe where theories and causes of action abound and one can spend days chasing down marginal arguments.

Traditional mediators are experts in what they do not need to know. They know or quickly learn the language and the context of the dispute and help focus everyone on the issues the parties see as crucial to agreement. These selected issues may become the entire focus of the mediation.

In advisory mediation of complex-fact cases such as construction, the parties must often go into much more detail in order to make the advice meaningful. Thus, processes which can take many days with advisory neutrals may take only a day or a few days with traditional mediators.

In the end, most people want to make their own deal, not the mediator's deal, although they may want the mediator to develop a range of options with them. With several options on the table acceptable to each side, the intensity of feeling about a particular outcome is lessened.

As a general rule, well-mediated negotiations don't blow up. Particularly in the political arena, non-mediated negotiations *do* blow up, bringing chaos where order is desperately needed. Consider the spotted owl controversy in the Pacific Northwest, where proposed regulations are driving private landowners to harvest their timber for fear of being prohibited from doing so.

Duration of the mediation. Traditional mediations may take longer in smaller cases and be faster in complex cases. This is because in simple disputes, giving advice is faster than helping the parties to find their own common ground. In complex matters, traditional mediation takes much less time, because of the mediator's lessened "need to know." A neutral not burdened with the need to give an opinion can more easily move the parties' focus to the most pivotal points and save days to weeks of process time.

Conclusion

The choice of mediator carries with it the choice of types of mediation. Pertinent questions include:

- **Is the problem an interpersonal one?** If so, traditional mediation is best.

- **Do you want an expert opinion?** Advisory mediation or traditional mediation with an advisory co-mediator is indicated.

- **Are you ready to listen to advice?** It is a mistake to use advisory mediation to persuade the other party, because advice-givers aren't that persuasive. A better test for the appropriateness of advisory mediation is, "Are you ready to seek advice?"

- **Are you primarily trying to get a handle on the case?** Traditional mediation is indicated.

- **Do you want a tough-minded mediator?** Both traditional and advisory mediation offer this, although it may be more common with advisory mediators.

- **Do you want a compassionate mediator?** Traditional mediators may be more likely to fill this bill.

- **Do you want an evaluation of your arguments and positions?** Both traditional and advisory mediation offer this, but with different emphasis. A traditional mediator is likely to present your weaknesses in confidential caucus as hurdles he sees. An advisory mediator is more likely to question your view, from the point of her expertise.

No mediator makes all clients happy. Every mediator will have some detractors and that's all right. The question is whether the detractors' complaints raise concerns that might be important in your situation.

Mediating is a highly complex activity that, when well-done, seems easy, even effortless. Poor mediators are very expensive, even if their services are free, because you lose an important opportunity to secure a high quality resolution.

Notes to Chapter 8

1. Linda R. Singer describes the situation well in her comprehensive and readable work, *Settling Disputes,* cited above (n. 4, Chap. 1) in the section "Mediation," pp. 20-25.

2. This is quoted in the excellent collection, *Dispute Resolution and Lawyers,* Leonard L. Riskin and James E. Westbrook (West Publishing Company), 1987, at p. 210. Second bracketed phrase added.

3. Eighty percent is a common figure used by mediation practitioners to describe convening and mediation successes, so long as their actual success rate equals or exceeds that figure.

4. This work was reported in 1988. Honeyman, "Five Elements of Mediation," *Negotiation Journal,* 4:149-158.

5. B. Honoroff, D. Matz and D. O'Connor, "Putting Mediation Skills to

the Test," *Negotiation Journal* 6:37-46.

6. SPIDR Commission on Qualifications, "Report: Qualifying Neutrals: The Basic Principles," 1989, National Institute for Dispute Resolution (NIDR).

7. The whole subject was reviewed at length and from many angles in a symposium published in the October, 1993, *Negotiation Journal.*

8. *Construction Mediation Booms,* Charles R. Schrader, Oregon State Bar Bulletin, February/March, 1992, p. 36.

9. As Robert A. Baruch-Bush puts it, "...the real challenge mediators face is not how to gain control of the agenda, but how to keep control in the *parties'* hands. The temptation for the mediator is to take control, rather than remaining committed to the principle of party control over the definition of the dispute." "Mixed Messages in the *Interim Guidelines,"* *Negotiation Journal,* 9:4, October, 1993, pp. 341-347

10. "Calls for Guidelines on Mediation," Wade Lambert, *Wall Street Journal,* October 22, 1993.

11. SPIDR (Society for Professionals in Dispute Resolution), headquartered in Washington, D.C., is a nationwide organization of neutrals, particularly arbitrators and mediators. Now 20 years old, this group is attempting to inform efforts around the country to define and restrict what mediators may do. Its charter is the protection of this infant profession so that it may evolve, unincumbered by narrow or misinformed regulation.

12. Thanks for this title to Richard A. Salem, "The *Interim Guidelines* Need A Broader Perspective," *Negotiation Journal,* 9:4, October, 1993, pp. 309-312.

13. See Chapter 10, *The Art of Mediating,* "The quality of space," for a further discussion on the readback.

14. Conversation with James Melamed, Professor of Negotiation and Mediation at University of Oregon Law School and Chair of the Oregon Dispute Resolution Commission February 15, 1994. He adds,

" 'Balance' describes how mediators do different things with different parties, depending on what they see as the need."

15. Prior to the *Interim Guidelines,* the term "invention" sparked intensive debate over the tilt toward a pro-active model of mediation. The phrase "generating options," does not imply the mediator should be launching proposals under his or her own banner. Using "what if" questions—What if the other side would agree to X?—to surface ideas is a good way of allowing the parties to reject the proposals or make them their own.

16. Deborah M. Kolb's early, thorough study of mediators in action, *The Mediators,* Massachusetts Institute of Technology, 1983, contains many useful observations on the process of mediating. See also her latest book, *When Talk Works*, Jossey-Bass, 1994.

17. Hippocrates stressed that surgeons should foster and use the healing power of nature rather than interfere unnecessarily. This is good counsel for mediators today, for the parties are the most knowledgeable about what it will take to resolve their differences. Humility dictates deference to the parties' wisdom, however hard it may be to bring it into play.

18. Some mediators reject the whole notion of making their own proposals. Others, advisory mediators in particular, see this as central to their role. My preference is for the mediator to use open-ended questions aimed at clarifying understanding in private caucus to develop the parties' thinking on the subject.

19. Testing is itself an arcane science. To date, the studies done on mediators have not yet been validated to standards recommended by the testing industry generally. *Interim Guidelines for Selecting Mediators* (NIDR), 1993, p. 3.

20. "Courts are a growing impetus for coming up with some standards." Prof. Frank E.A. Sander, Harvard Law School. "When courts encourage mediation, there must be some assurance that there are qualified individuals involved," from n. 10, "Calls Increase for Guidelines on Mediation," Lambert. The headline of this article is somewhat misleading. The reporter found only one instance of complaint against a

mediator and quoted no one outside of the profession who was seeking, actively, to encourage the establishment of mediator standards. The work of Christopher Honeyman, Professor Sander and the Test Design Project is focused on finding out what, exactly, mediators do in order to begin to define competence for the profession.

21. See n. 19, Interim Guidelines for Selecting Mediators, NIDR, at p. 1.

22. See Carrie Menkel-Meadow, "Measuring Both the Art and Science of Mediation," *Negotiation Journal,* 9:4, October, 1993, pp. 321-325; David E. Matz, "Some Advice for Mediator Evaluators," *Negotiation Journal,* 9:4, October, 1993, pp. 327-330.

23. For a justification of an expert level of "substantive knowledge," see George H. Friedman and Allan D. Silberman, "A Useful Tool for Evaluating Potential Mediators," *Negotiation Journal,* 9:4, October, 1993, pp. 313-315. What the authors overlook in their enthusiasm for subject area expertise (such as lawyers or engineers rather than mediators, for example, might have) is that traditional mediators who are process experts are able to move much more rapidly to what the parties see as critical, because they are not encumbered by their own professional opinions.

24. Both have done much to advance the use of litigation alternatives, AAA by focusing on arbitration and CPR by focusing on minitrial. CPR's Jim Henry wrote years ago of mediation as "the sleeping giant." Henry and Lieberman, *The Manager's Guide to Resolving Legal Disputes: Better Results without Litigation,* 1985.

25. These mediators were trained in traditional mediation, where the essential skills are in the mediation process, not in giving advice. In such mediation, the mediator's non-mediation training and experience are not so relevant as her current skills and abilities. See Honoroff, Matz & O'Connor, "Putting Mediation Skills to the Test," *Negotiation Journal,* cited above (n. 5).

26. Advisory mediation is not to be confused with "muscle mediation" in which the mediator becomes an advocate for his position. Muscle mediation is not really mediation at all.

27. See note 26, above. In 1540, during the reign of Henry VIII, the organization of the Company of Barber Surgeons of London marked the beginning of some control in qualifications for performing operations. This guild, which lasted 200 years, was the precursor of the Royal College of Surgeons of London.

9.
PREPARING TO MEDIATE

Everything an Indian does is in a circle, and that is because the power of the world always works in circles and everything tries to be round.
— Nicholas Black Elk, *Black Elk Speaks,* as told to John J. Neihardt (1961)

Mediation preparation begins with an analysis of objectives. They must be framed specifically, not just in terms of dollars. They must be realistic yet held lightly, always subject to review based on new information and fresh perspective.

The decision to resolve, or not, should take into account the hazards of litigation. Most often, frustration and aggravation do not translate into the bottom line.

After analysis comes implementation: what will it take to get what you want? What information and people and what kind of presentation, what kind of negotiation strategies are needed to best assure the desired outcome? What goes around, comes around.

Who Should Attend?

Preparation begins with the question, "Who should attend?" Having the right people present is key to mediation's success. Sometimes, lawyers and others make themselves more available for court procedures than for mediation. That is a mistake. It says litigation is more important than mediation. Nothing is more important than for decision-makers to be present at a mediation.

This is one of the clearest rules about mediation.

The need for counsel in mediation varies. Family mediation is often done without lawyers present. However, this has become controversial where there is any question of a party's ability to negotiate.[1] In commercial mediation where litigation is "in the picture," there seems to be general agreement lawyers should participate. If it is decided not to have lawyers participate, then it is important to assure that any lawyer whose advice you are listening to at the time be kept informed on the mediation. This means allowing the lawyer to advise you going into the mediation and perhaps having the lawyer on standby during the mediation, available to take your call, if needed. It may mean having the lawyer come when an agreement is reached, so that a proper memorandum can be drawn up. See Chapter 5, *Lawyers at the Threshold* and Appendix 2, *Writing Agreements in Mediation.*

Others whose presence is desirable may include spouses and perhaps other members of the decision-maker's family, where they have substantial influence. Claims supervisors might be needed. Experts whose information or reactions are important may be needed in person or on telephone standby. Sometimes key witnesses are held in reserve, for possible telephone interview.

With the decision about whose presence is needed comes the decision about whose presence is likely to be destructive. Sometimes a party's negotiating team includes an individual who will lose face if that side's position is compromised. To increase the chances of success, assess the liabilities as well as the assets of potential negotiating team members from your own and the other side.

Case example: unmaking an enemy. Owhy Corp. had a contract claim against a federal government agency. The official who made the adverse decision was the principal decider on the company's appeal. He had again denied its claim, and claims litigation was begun. This individual still had weight with the agency. What could the company do?

If Owhy had an enemy, this man was it. Everyone was

powerless to get rid of him. At the suggestion of a mediator serving as settlement consultant, company executives began to ask themselves exactly what value this individual represented to the other side and looked for a higher value which would permit them to get paid. The obstacle was studied from the perspective of "how does it serve?"

Could it be, for example, that the value this person represented was that of not paying excessive and unjust claims? Everyone in the agency would agree with that value. So long as that individual was seen as speaking for that value, he would continue to have influence. If, however, the company could identify another important value which would be threatened by that individual's participation in the mediation, it could get a fairer hearing.

In casual meetings with agency counsel, the company's attorney emphasized that value — the value of paying just claims promptly — as part of making agency counsel aware of the strength of his case. When it came to discussing who the most constructive negotiation team members from each side would be, the obstacle's name wasn't mentioned. The claim was successfully negotiated at the ensuing mediation.

Convening

What causes the mediation to occur? It doesn't just happen. It is the end product of steps taken by counsel, parties and the mediator or mediation firm. Each is a co-creator of the mediation itself. The first stage is convening.

Attracting people to the mediation table. Some view convening as insignificant. The preliminaries aren't as glamorous as the mediation itself. In the early years, new firms in the Alternative Dispute Resolution (ADR) market offered convening services, sometimes called "bringing the parties to the table," free. They quickly found that there was a lot more to it than they imagined and very few cases ever got to the table; they languished in the

ADR firm's file drawer. As one old claims adjuster in Minneapolis observed wryly, "I wish someone would pay *me* $100 a case (the filing fee then) to keep these cases in *my* file drawer."

The quality of the convening bears fruit in the mediation itself. It is true that attracting people to mediation is more complicated than relying on compulsory attendance by rule or order of court. It is also more beneficial. In writing the letters and making the telephone calls to convene the parties, you open participants to more creative approaches. They become more hopeful about reaching resolution, an advantage when the going gets tough later on.

Convening requires listening and speaking skills, and both a goal and process orientation. Frontal assault on resistance is ineffectual, for participation must be voluntary if mediation is to deliver even a fraction of what it has to offer. This is one of the reasons why court-ordered mediation often seems so burdensome to parties. Energy is invested in resistance, not in exploring the possibilities constructively.

Using the mediator to convene the mediation. Remember: *you* do not need to get the other side to agree to mediate. Convening is often done by the mediator you select or the mediation firm's case manager. A third-party invitation sidesteps impasses which have already developed between the parties. The success rate in convening using professional mediators or case managers is above eighty percent, so the odds are good if you choose this course. For those who choose to do their own convening, a discussion of various techniques may be helpful.

Doing your own convening. When you convene a mediation, you are inviting others to participate in a remarkable process. It is unstructured, but can be given structure as needed. It is personal but not dangerously confrontational, by virtue of the mediator's presence and role. It is sometimes helpful to think of convening as inviting people to a party or game. Yes, there's this serious situation, but let's roll up our sleeves, be a bit more tolerant of each other and give it our best. In game mode, it is less stressful to handle the initial rejection and any stray verbal shots. *Think of rejection as only an initial rejection, signifying no more than that something else needs to be done before mediation can take place.*

The skills of a convener are those of a negotiator, for convening is itself a negotiation. The object of convening is simply to bring the parties together with at least enough interest to stay a while. You don't need any commitments other than to show up. It works even if people come just because they are curious.

Convening skills. Careful listening helps one hear between the lines. Many people are word-oriented, taking words at face value. When someone says they are not interested in mediation, that's that.

In one joint telephone conference with two counsel during a convening, a mediator had occasion to talk to one of them after the other got off the line.

"You see," the lawyer said, "no dice."

"I wouldn't be so hasty," the mediator said. "I believe the proposal will fly, it simply needs some fine tuning."

"But I heard him say 'no,' " the lawyer insisted.

"I heard that too," the mediator said, "but it wasn't a final 'no.' You have room to maneuver."

The case settled in mediation not long thereafter.

The skilled negotiator looks beyond the words to the context in which they are spoken, the tone of voice, even the assumptions on which the statements are based. What is the underlying cause of resistance?

Listening with a judgmental attitude is worthless for this purpose. Getting self-righteous and muttering, "They'll never listen," sets up a self-fulfilling prophecy. The need to be right is often so strong that people would rather lose the opportunity to mediate than be wrong about their opponent's resistance. Not surprisingly, they often do lose.

Listening skills and strategic thinking are tools of the negotiator. An example of how they are used is a recently convened mediation of a construction case.

Case example: winning the judge's support. In this eight-party case, one party was reluctant to commit to mediating. The case manager talked with other key counsel in the case about how they might use the upcoming court status conference. They decided to mention the interest in mediating to the judge. The strategy worked. The judge took a substantial interest in the proposed mediation and set the next status conference for one week after the mediation date. "I want to hear all about the mediation," the judge concluded. After that, the reluctant party agreed to participate.

There was no need to accuse the reluctant party before the court. That strong-arm tactic would have been a weaker strategy, since the court would not have compelled attendance at mediation. Mentioning the upcoming mediation to the court put pressure on the reluctant lawyer. He did not want to have to explain at the next status conference why his client did not participate. He left the hearing with his options intact, persuaded that it was in his client's best interests to participate.

Verbal strategies and skills. The verbal skills used to convene a negotiation are quite different from the verbal skills of advocacy. In negotiation and mediation, you use words to acknowledge feelings and to affirm factual assertions and arguments. Verbal skills help you give back to the speaker a version of what they have said which minimizes the dead-end, destructive comments you have heard and emphasizes those that were creative and constructive.

You respond to the dead-end observations at the feeling level. You acknowledge the feelings the speaker is expressing, rather than the words of the communication. This tells the speaker he or she has been heard and understood.

When you respond directly to the words by arguing, this convinces the speaker that you aren't capable of hearing what they are saying. To reason with a person who doesn't listen obviously will be fruitless. And so the discussion goes nowhere.

Here are some sample exchanges that might occur during an invitation to mediate. The comments which follow provide insight into the dynamics of these telephone communications. Test your own reactions to what is being said on both sides.

Sample Invitation

I've been thinking. Maybe it would be useful to try mediation at this point. We know the rough outlines of the situation. It's going to take a lot of work, time and money to do the needed discovery to refine this very much more. What if we sit down with our counsel and a mediator and see what we can accomplish?

Take the invitation apart, piece by piece:

I've been thinking.

(Indicates an interest in working creatively toward resolution. It can catch an opponent off-guard.)

Maybe it would be useful to try mediation at this point.

(You sound tentative — though your resolve may be made of steel — in order to invite a productive discussion rather than an argument.)

We know the rough outlines of the situation. It's going to take a lot of work, time and money to do the needed discovery to refine this very much more.

(This general justification for the idea of mediating invites a discussion. It puts you both on the same side, with a mutual interest in the efficient resolution of differences. It establishes the area of common interest; from there you can pick off issues which divide you.)

What if we sit down with a mediator and see what we can accomplish?

("What if" is the classic way of forwarding an idea without ownership. This enables the listener to make it his or her own idea and gets authorship off the table as a possibly divisive issue.)

That's a good start. But the real work begins with what follows.

Response #1: Rejection Based on Perception of the Merits

There's really nothing to mediate. I just don't think you have a case.

(There are many ways to respond to what is wisely considered the *initial rejection.* Here are some of them.)

Initiator: Acknowledgment; Opening the Discussion

I know you really believe in your position.

(Responds to the feeling of frustration, but avoids an argument about whether or not there is something to mediate.)

And you know I've been committed to mine. Maybe there's something we've overlooked. If one or the other of us is wrong, I'd sure rather know now than later.

(There are several things here the opposing party will agree with. One of them is the idea that you may have overlooked something. You also follow up with a practical observation that if someone doesn't have a case and finds out early, a lot of wasted effort is saved. This reinforces the idea that you are open to reason.)

What have we got to lose by spending a few hours in mediation?

(Discussion is still open. You have provided food for thought; if you don't get agreement now, you may get it later. You've also put mediation in perspective, by showing that few resources are involved in trying it out.)

Response #2: Rejection Based on Personal Considerations

I think your side isn't being honest. What's the use of talking when there is so little trust?

Initiator: Opening the Discussion

Well, we can agree right now to try this case and forget the possibility of resolving it ourselves at a lot less cost in time and money.

(This is the consequence of holding the view expressed. Often a person doesn't realize that views such as this mean, literally, that there will never be anything to talk about.)

Or we can see what the possibilities are. With mediation, it's a lot easier to deal with people issues like this. And we can negotiate about whatever certainty is needed to conclude an agreement.

(You discuss the implications of this serious lack of trust specifically, to see if you can get behind the categorical statement to a place where reason will prevail.)

We're only talking about a few hours of our time.

(Again, you put mediation in perspective.)

Response #3: Rejection Based on Timing

This case isn't ready to settle yet. What's the point?

(The assumption is obviously that mediation is only useful when it's time to settle. Yet much time and money can be saved by using mediation to secure agreements on procedures which will lead to settlement.)

Initiator: Acknowledges, Gives New Information, Lays Groundwork for Follow-up

You may be right.

(This is one of your most useful phrases. It admits nothing, but is read by your listener as a sure sign you are hearing and understanding what they are saying.)

But I've been surprised in several situations that cases I knew wouldn't settle in mediation, did.

(Shows empathy with their viewpoint, yet provides new information about how perceptions are often erroneous.)

Also, we've got these expert issues on the horizon. If we just got together to look for a better way of handling them, it would be worthwhile.

(Gives something specific to focus on, rather than generalities. Also, you are in prime time to persuade. Once a person knows he has been heard and understood, he is far more receptive to what is being offered.)

I don't know about you, but I would rather not make a career out of this case.

(In litigation the other side is often convinced that you want to drag out the case. It is a strategic decision whether and when to disabuse them of this idea. In discussions around mediation, this impression can serve as additional reason that mediation might be helpful. Also, it serves to remind opposing counsel of his own client's needs and interests, something it is all too easy to overlook in the pressures of litigation.)

Strategic Preparation

Since mediation works to secure agreement on what you need and how you're going to get it, you need only prepare appropriately. With almost no preparation, you might take a run at settling a case you consider worth little more than nuisance value or one in which you feel the parties are not so far apart. If this does not result in resolution, you could agree to resume at another date, after identifying what each side will do to prepare for further mediation. Nothing is lost, and indeed much is gained, by setting the negotiation process in motion.

On the eve of trial or in a situation where you anticipate there will be no opportunity for another mediation session, you might want to prepare more extensively. Or you may prepare strategically, focusing on what you think will be most important and having the rest of the information accessible, if not on the tip of your tongue. On the other hand, you may want to save the expense of preparation, as one San Francisco lawyer who handles construction disputes and is very experienced in the use of traditional mediation. He advises his clients:

> You should prepare for the mediation as little as possible. The reason for this is that you conserve costs and you can control the mediation process anyway. If an issue comes up that you're not prepared for, you can break and go do the necessary work to deal with it.[2]

Advisory mediation is less amenable to this flexible approach, but it could still be used to improve cost-effectiveness, with the advance concurrence of the mediator. Forewarned, the mediator will not be expecting to give his opinion before it is timely.

Use the mediator. A major resource in the preparation phase of the mediation is your mediator. Some mediators offer confidential discussion opportunities to each side before the mediation. These may be in person or by telephone. Often, in a relatively short time, perhaps half an hour, you can get a host of useful perspectives on how to use the mediation most effectively.

If you have been immersed in adversarial processes, you may think initially that the one you prepare to persuade is the judge or jury. In mediation, it is the other side you must persuade. Each side must find some benefit in the outcome or they will not buy into it. The mediator's experience is extremely useful in helping you to shift your thought processes to persuading the other side.

Another use of the mediator is to build congruent expectations on both sides about what will happen in the mediation. He may help assure that, where the parties so desire, each side is prepared to meet and receive what the other is saying. For example, if one side is going to bring an expert, the other side better have their expert present, to help evaluate the presentation.

Plan to use the mediator or mediation firm for all discussions about what will happen in the mediation. Either in private or joint preliminary session or by telephone, you can talk with the mediator about what type of presentation and approach will be most effective and what you and the other side need to know in order to evaluate settlement options. This discussion may touch on experts, audiovisual aids, and witnesses who could be useful either as part of the presentation or in reserve. The discussion will help establish the critical focus on persuasion rather than argument. In mediation, no one wins unless an outcome is agreed on.

Negotiating without the mediator about issues to be discussed can consume a great deal of time. Counsel with little mediation experience have a tendency to over-structure the discussions, rather than taking advantage of mediation's flexibility.

The benefit of the mediator's experience is also lost.

Suspend disbelief. You can improve your odds of success in mediation by being willing to believe, however briefly, that you will succeed in reaching agreement. A good mediation causes this to happen spontaneously. Within a short time, you begin to *act and speak* as though it were going to succeed. You can see the mediator deal with difficulties and notice that a pattern of agreements is being developed. You will help to devise a framework for working out differences and see the benefit of the parties' receiving positive reinforcement for their successes. You and the others become more creative, more reasonable and the discussion becomes more a problem-solving exercise than an exercise in futility.

Evaluate information needs. A key item on your pre-mediation checklist is information. It is part of your mediation tool kit. If you are going to a mediation to settle the matter, be sure to bring the information you will need to support your arguments and calculations. Look at the information needs of *both* parties. Specifically, do you have what you need to evaluate settlement options? If not, should you try to get it before or during mediation? Ask yourself the same questions about the other side.

Seek mutuality. One's own readiness is useless if the other side is not adequately informed. This is a key strategy. Once again, things have to work for all or they work for none. How many times have I heard one counsel say, "Yes, he was calling me about those documents all the time, but they weren't very important to me and it was a lot of trouble. I was too busy." Often those are the very documents that would have enabled the other side to evaluate settlement options and were crucial to getting the requester to agree with the foot-dragging counsel's view of the case.

Use surprise sparingly. Surprise needs to be carefully evaluated. If the surprise relates to something which stands on its own and does not invite inquiry, it is good to use it in the mediation. As an example, see Chapter 7, "The Silver Bullet." If, however, it is something which cries for further investigation, think carefully about whether or not to disclose it in advance so that the other side will be prepared to respond to it. It is fine to use surprise, but have in mind that insurance carriers, in particular, react poorly to surprise. The more complex the decision-making structure on the other side, the more hazardous is surprise.

Where insurance carriers are involved in big cases, the person with authority to substantially increase the reserves on a claim may be back at the home office. Many of these close at 4 p.m. eastern time. If you wait until afternoon to introduce new information that substantially raises the ante in a case, particularly in the western states, you may have lost the opportunity to have the mediator working on both sides' perceptions of the value of that information. There is a sense of urgency that builds in mediation. Take advantage of it.

Assess the timing and extent of disclosure. In planning pre-mediation or mediation-session disclosures, there are degrees of openness. You have exceedingly fine control over the flow of information in mediation. Information can be presented, insinuated about, leaked, or withheld.

Decide the timing of providing information in the mediation itself based on what is going on. What is to be gained? What might be lost? How receptive is the opponent? Does the mediator need this information to penetrate the other side's thinking on the issue? The tendency in mediation is to inform rather than hold back for the simple reason that most information is truly necessary for the parties to sufficiently close the gap in their views in order to reach an agreement. You make these decisions moment by moment as the mediation proceeds.

Construction mediations, for example, usually involve active participation by the principals so that some joint understanding can be built, piece by piece, out of the experience and recollection of the parties. The mediator keeps this information-giving in balance. When a party feels they are giving all of the information, they see it as giving up power and feel taken advantage of. This destroys trust and threatens the viability of the mediation.

Forms And Modes Of Presentation

There are many ways of presenting information in mediation. Chief among them is the oral presentation.

Your oral presentation. Mediation is an oral process. Enjoy it. Think of yourself as a good storyteller. Since the story, ultimately, must persuade not the mediator but the other side, be gracious and generous in your story. And be relevant. Venting is all right, but dumping is not. If your side's situation resembles the Augean Stables,[3] cluster and group items so as not to seem to be presenting a litany of grievances.

Your oral presentation is the way you position yourself in the mediation. It is important to organize it either chronologically or in some other logical fashion. When making the statement, include all important parts of your position. Don't simply assume your listeners remember everything in your written presentation. Even if they did, they would not give it the emphasis you do. If some points are covered in detail in a written submission, briefly summarize them in your oral pres-entation so the flow and meaning of your presentation is clear.

Remember that your audience is the other side. The mediator is a translator and interpreter of your position to the other side and vice versa. Give him something to work with, even if you believe the other side knows every bit of it already.

Your opening may run from a few minutes to several hours, depending on the case. As soon as you have finished, some mediators will concisely and elegantly summarize what you have said in a readback, so be prepared to decide whether that summary is accurate and complete.

Verbal Information. Information from witnesses or those responsible for the operation of systems can be very powerful.

Sometimes, as in construction mediation, this information is given by individuals through their ongoing participation in the discussion. But even non-participants have a chance to tell what they know in a coherent and orderly fashion.

The mediator sets the stage as a quest for information. The qualities of an adversarial process are minimized. When additional information is needed by an opposing party, the mediator usually asks the questions. This eliminates the lawyering of the questions that could turn a simple inquiry into a fully adversarial process. An expert may be required to state his qualifications and any reasonable question is fair. The neutrality of questioning allows the witnesses to look as good as they can so that the mediator's reactions, given privately and later, will be meaningful.

Another way of offering information is to have a witness available on telephone standby. Offering a witness for an off-the-record interview shows openness as well as confidence. Imagine that you have negotiated to a point where it is obvious that someone to whom you have access has the key information everyone needs to be able to move forward. You lean forward and say: "If you like, you can find out right now. So-and-so is available on telephone standby. We have a speaker phone here. Let the mediator make the call and ask the questions. Let's see what happens."

Sometimes, the opposing side refuses what seems to be a golden opportunity for fear it is being set up or because it doesn't feel prepared. The point has been made perhaps better than the witness could make it. When the questioning does proceed, a lot of erroneous supposition can quickly be laid to rest. If you are the one surprised by such an offer, ask for a caucus, invite the mediator, and go along with the interview if you can. You can always put what is said in context, if you don't like it. And you may find it not so bitter a pill as you fear.

Documents and summaries. When you anticipate that the mediation will be fact-intensive, it is good to have key documents or important summaries at hand. People rarely see the same thing in documents, so your ability to pinpoint the support for your assertions can have great weight. This is particularly true when the evidence is unequivocal.

Rules, regulations and decisions. When a rule, regulation or decision is important to your side, have it there in full text. Highlighting may be helpful. Let the mediator review it before plunging into extensive argument about its meaning. Then you will get more benefit from the mediator's confidential reaction.

Written submissions. At times, it is helpful to make a written submission to the mediator in advance of the mediation. If the facts are unduly complicated or a new or novel issue requires briefing, by all means do so. Sometimes providing the mediator with copies of pertinent papers already filed in court is sufficient. Or you may want to prepare new material. Any submission may be shared with the other side, or at your option be entirely confidential, something the other side has not seen and will not see.

These submissions may run from a few pages to several bankers' boxes. Remember that mediation is an oral process. It is usually best to make the presentation orally, rather than relying on written material. Otherwise, you deprive the mediator of a lot of material he or she needs to get the mediation off on the right track. See Chapter 10, *The Art of Mediating,* "Quality of Space."

Settlement agreement drafts. Many kinds of settlements fall into well-defined patterns for documentation: a dismissal with prejudice by the plaintiff of the lawsuit; a full release of the defendants and a fairly spare settlement agreement, outlining who has agreed to do what and when, perhaps with required statutory language. It saves a great deal of time later on to bring drafts of the "boiler plate," legal language commonly used, drawn in as neutral language as possible, with appropriate blanks. Laptop computers, also, are valuable, particularly in settings where a fully equipped office is not available. See Appendix 2, *Writing Agreements Reached in Mediation.*

Preparing Yourself

You come to mediation for the sole purpose of seeing whether it is possible to reach some resolution that meets your needs. If that is impossible, you should be prepared to explore what information each side might need to be better able to evaluate settlement options. You need to be able to listen well, to reflect wisely and to make decisions.

Disputes create a kind of stress or compression in us. Common phrases like "he's sure wound up," and "she always works under a head of steam," speak to this stressful compression. Most people bring this right into the mediation. The mediator will do all he can to allow it to be safely diffused, but you can help with this process. For an exercise to relieve the stress or compression of the dispute and become far more effective in mediation, see Appendix 1, *Decompression Exercise.*

Conclusion

Convening and preparing for a mediation offer many opportunities for strategy. Keep the strategy constructive by focusing on mutuality — making common cause with the other side, looking for mutual gain, like Black Elk who understood the circularity of everything we do. If you're not ready to do this, put the matter aside and come back to it when you're fresher. Your perspective is crucial.

Notes to Chapter 9

1. See the article by Trina Grillo, in Chapter 1 at n. 4.

2. See Chapter 5, n. 8, a speech by Lee Novich. For situations where extensive preparation is always required, see Chapter 13, *Charting Public and Private Policy.*

3. In Greek mythology, the Augean Stables were owned by Augeas, king of Elis, in Greece. 3,000 oxen occupied the stables, which had not been cleaned in 30 years. One of the labors of Hercules, son of Jupiter and a human mother, was to clean them in a day. He did so by diverting and joining two rivers to run through the stables, leaving them entirely clean in only one day.

10.
THE ART OF MEDIATING

Why not go out on a limb? That's where the fruit is. — Will Rogers

Making It Work: The Human Side

We have watched the game of mediation from the grandstand. Now let's look at the inner life of mediation, what is happening beneath the surface. Mediation is much more enjoyable when you do your part. It isn't just about settling a dispute. It's about changing people's relationships to the problem and to each other. The people side of the equation is as important as the legal and factual sides.

Mediation is the process but satisfaction is the goal. We often make the mistake of defining our goal as battlefield victory, assuming that this will satisfy our interests. We keep plugging away until we achieve the goal, even if it be a Pyrrhic victory, or until we find it impossible to achieve. Dogged determination of this type is not appropriate in mediation. In mediation, there is an opportunity to re-examine goals as well as strategies to see if the way they have been defined ignores realities and imposes needless burdens on our securing satisfaction. Goals need adjustment from time to time until achieving them satisfies our true interests.

The goal of satisfying our underlying interests is a worthy one. To achieve it, we entertain various hypotheses about what it will take, without being captured by them. Success is more likely when we are open to the myriad forms in which satisfaction may come rather than being locked on to one form only.

The mediator's balancing role. Some critics fear that a party will enter mediation with a strong hand, only to have the mediator bail out the weaker party. One experience with mediation will put this fallacy to rest. Mediation is too dependent on trust to get very far with high-handed tactics.[1]

The term "power-balancing" is not entirely accurate. It is not positions that are balanced in mediation, but the ability to participate equally in a negotiation. Power in most marriages, for example, is exercised differently, but is nonetheless balanced. While one spouse has the power of speaking, the other has the power of silence. While one understands finances, the other understands emotions. The divorce arena provides considerable insight into the concept of power-balancing.

Good divorce mediators, for example, generally work to balance negotiating power between the parties. This tends to produce agreements that are voluntary, rather than coerced. With a stake in keeping the agreements, both sides are more likely to live up to them.

The mediator may therefore encourage the silent party to speak or the speaking party to become silent, to educate one about finances and the other about emotions. This breaks the power system on which the marriage was based and empowers the parties by moving them out of their dependency.

Sometimes, a party is unaware of the power they wield and fails to take responsibility for outcomes. Good mediators frequently have an understanding about where real power lies and they use this awareness to assure that we look at the long- and intermediate-term consequences as well as the immediate effects of our position.[2]

In advisory mediation, the advisor's expertise automatically balances the parties positions to some extent. A weak negotiator has less risk, since there is a "neutral" measurer of fairness. Power-balancing in certain other situations may be necessary when the parties are unrepresented or counsel are not personally present. Without two parties capable of negotiating, mediation must be terminated.

Experienced negotiators want to be sure there is someone on the other side capable of negotiating. In one case, a distraught plaintiff in a wrongful termination case fired her lawyer midway through a mediation.[3] She then asked to meet privately with the lead defense counsel. There was a risk the mediation might have to be terminated because of the plaintiff's distraught condition. The mediator, the plaintiff's former counsel and defense counsel discussed ways of helping the plaintiff see it was in her own best interest to continue with her counsel, who had been doing a good job under very difficult circumstances. After a brief, private conversation with defense counsel, the plaintiff asked to meet with the mediator and scoped out the reinstatement of her lawyer. The mediation proceeded to a conclusion with which both she and her former employer were satisfied.

Mediation may reveal that power is not where we suppose. Sometimes the apparently powerful party is utterly dependent on the seemingly weaker party. The weaker party refuses to take responsibility for the power he or she holds, and the parties remain deadlocked.

In commercial mediation, power-balancing may be addressed to either side, or both. For example, in one wrongful termination case in Chicago, the plaintiff, a bright, older black man, was mentally disturbed and had managed in his brief time with the company to humiliate most of the top brass and disrupt shareholder relations. He came to the mediation with his third lawyer, having discharged the previous two. The company felt it held all the cards. Nevertheless, the plaintiff was continuing to cause a lot of embarrassment.

The mediator suggested to the corporate defendant that beating someone mentally impaired wasn't much of an accomplishment. The company might better satisfy its interest in justice by working for a compassionate resolution. It turned out that an employee mental health benefit program was available, so the company became willing to think in terms of a rehabilitative settlement. The mediator then appealed to the plaintiff, the apparently weaker party, to put the fight into the context of the rest of his life and then decide how much to sacrifice now in pursuing revenge. He finally began to let go of his vendetta, as a settlement that met his needs was hammered out by his counsel and counsel for the defendant.

Because resolution requires mutual approval, people eventually put aside the one-sided view that for them to win, the other side must lose. This is the beginning of problem-solving and often the beginning of a negotiated resolution.

The quality of space. Good mediators can create and hold the quality environment needed to make rapid progress in any kind of negotiation. It is more than an atmosphere.

When a high quality space has been created, the parties become absorbed in the process of resolving their differences. Some mediators give few breaks and no time for lunch — food is brought in. The intensity and focus promote resolution without hardship, because everyone's attention is fully on the subject.

Creating and holding a safe, high quality space requires mediator attentiveness to subtle shifts in power balance, confidence, a participant's trust in the process, feeling states, and in ability to present one's side or to hear and comprehend the other's. Mediators use many tools to make this happen. One is *the readback*, a succinct restatement of the information given by a party following its presentation.

An expert readback acknowledges the constructive portions of a party's presentation but responds to the feelings behind angry or destructive words. In it, the mediator shapes his own observations, responses and restatement in such a way as to allow the various parties to hear what has been said and to clarify the focus. A half-hour presentation can be summarized in a readback as a clearer and more cogent synopsis in perhaps two or three minutes. The technique is an art form in the hands of expert mediators and sets the stage for the entire mediation.

The quality of space is what allows people to relax, to put the accumulated hurts aside and become constructive. It is what encourages the transformation of the parties' relationship from adversarial to problem-solving, and it is the hallmark of a high-quality mediator. Parties, absorbed in the conflict, may not recognize it early in the mediation. At times, they never do, but they nevertheless get the benefit.

Getting to feelings. Mediation is the time to bring out the best that is in us. This does not mean to put on a false front. Nothing is more transparent than smiles that fade the minute the person takes their eyes off us. Courtesy, consideration for others, compassion (feeling with), dignity and presence (attention) are all qualities that win not only points but a better result.[4]

Inevitably, there are gaps in the process when the mediator is caucusing with another party and we do not have a specific or general assignment. It is tempting to fall into story-telling, running down the opposition or parking ourselves by the telephone to deal with other matters. Such activities are often interpreted by the other parties as lack of commitment to the process, no matter how hard we have worked previously. However, bringing a good book we can read behind our papers isn't likely to get us into trouble.

When the process shifts into low gear, people start working harder to see if there isn't some way to reach a mutually satisfactory resolution. One side's serious consideration of proposals and head-scratching about alternatives is a sign of respect for the other side and vice-versa. Good mediators will be acknowledging all sides' sincere efforts to make progress, in part because there is such effort and in part to encourage deeper commitment. It is usually a self-fulfilling prophecy: by expecting the best they draw out the best.

Both sides may have a lot of feeling tied up in the dispute. Mediation allows this to be expressed in joint session, in private caucus with the mediator and in private talks with counsel. The key to success in joint sessions is to honor those feelings by acknowledging them. No matter how angry the words, considerate response to the feelings underlying them will let the person know that he has been heard and understood.

Counsel may also have a lot of feelings tied up in a matter. Tensions between counsel encumber the entire process. By keeping calm, you can seize the opportunity you might otherwise have missed. Consider this example which demonstrates how appropriate humor may produce a change in atmosphere.

Case example: counsel wrangle resolved. This seven-party California construction case involved two counsel who truly hated each other. One defense lawyer had filed motions to have the other removed from the case, due to being a witness to some events under consideration. The plaintiff's lawyer had retaliated with complaints to the bar association about this counsel's conduct. Their warring was poisoning everyone's efforts toward settlement.

The mediation got off to a rocky start and the main agreement was to convene a second day of mediation in the plaintiff's home town. The plaintiff's chief counsel was host. All the other lawyers had to travel some distance to get to the second day of mediation. The morning session went slowly, in part due to the atmosphere contributed by the two warring counsel.

At lunch, the group was taken to a nearby club. When the two arrived, late, there were only two empty seats, side by side at the round dining table. During the lunch, the two managed to stumble through passing the salt and pepper, the butter, the rolls, and the coffee, to the others' well-masked amusement. As the group walked back to the conference room, a gentle humor broke out and the two began to let go of some of their hostility.

During the afternoon session, the two began to be constructive. The mediator congratulated them and the others on their good efforts. Momentum to settle began to build. The case settled in a third day of mediation.

It's always darkest just before dawn. In the nature of things, hurdles in mediation sometimes appear insurmountable. You are tempted to walk out. What reason could there be for staying, with the other side being so intransigent? Watch and wait. The mediator knows where the discussions are hung up and may become pretty blunt with you, with the other side or with both sides. Allow time for that all to take effect. People and perspectives change, but this takes time. The mediator equivalent to a body block is to step between you and the door and plead for a little more time, to allow the process to work. This is how President Carter brought about the Camp David accord.[5]

Opportunities for reconciliation. Once agreement is reached, counsel will often work then and there to hammer out the terms of the written agreement. This process is described in Appendix 2. While counsel are drafting agreements, the clients may be getting back on speaking terms. The mediator may sit in at these casual moments, to get the discussion going. At the conclusion of one construction mediation, the parties, both businessmen, gave the mediator a standing ovation. Even former employees who sue their employers may become, after a successful mediation, constructive members of the employer's loyal alumni.

There is time for talk about plans for the future. Future-thinking is often blocked by the weight and demands of the dispute. This kind of talk is a healthy sign that the dispute is being left behind, so each person can move on to new things.

Building Power

Misconceptions of power.[6] Power is often thought of as manipulating or as synonymous with force. Force is a crude form of power and underlies much of our collective bargaining processes.[7] It is based on the assumption that for us to win, the other side must lose, an odd operating guideline for a relationship.

In fact, *power is the ability to get one's desires satisfied.* Authority is the coercive force that depends on one's position to get others to do things whether they like it or not. It is far weaker than true power, which inspires people to join in common cause with the holder of power for mutual benefit.[8]

Mediation's role. Mediation plays into the important American value of resolving matters ourselves. The remedies available in mediation are limited only by our imagination. Often, those items with little or no monetary value prove critical to final agreement. People routinely agree in mediation to do things no court would compel them to do, for they see that these agreements serve their own underlying interests as well as satisfying the other side.

Interest-satisfaction is what determines the quality of the resolution. Interests are what lie behind what people say they want. Both a plaintiff's demand for a seven figure settlement (one million dollars or more) and our spouse's demand for a new car spring from underlying interests, not necessarily greed or ostentation. This means that satisfaction can often be secured by something different from the demand, provided those underlying interests are met.

We battle under banners proclaiming *rights,* yet these are rarely clear. Often they are contradictory. It is the quality of our legal system to maintain many separate and conflicting threads of decisional law and practice simultaneously. Rights are determined by a tribunal which considers the peculiar facts of the situation and decides which body of authority applies to it. When rights are agreed to, however, they provide a shorthand way of making decisions. Problems then arise only at the periphery of the rights.

Negotiating to resolve a dispute always takes place in the context of rights and power, defined and undefined. Perhaps it is because rights are fuzzy, once the factual situation emerges, that people so overwhelmingly choose to design their own resolutions. Or perhaps certainty is a sufficient motivator for most of us.

Mediation empowers us to satisfy our underlying interests. Mediators often influence parties to drop strategies that jerk others around in favor of those that serve mutual needs. This does not diminish that side's power. It enhances their ability to get something they want. Mediators thus help parties to understand that apparent power is different from real power and to see how they are participating in perpetuating the problem.

We always have a choice about whether to resolve or not. If there is no agreement, the mediation has not failed. The mediator has not failed. William F. Lincoln, one of the pioneers in the mediation field and a pre-eminent teacher of mediation skills and techniques, has said:

> The mediator never fails. It is the parties who reach or fail to reach an agreement. When they exercise that choice, they are doing exactly what mediation was created to allow them to do.[9]

Notes to Chapter 10

1. Complaints about pressure tactics may be more common in advisory mediations, where the neutral gives an opinion and then may become overly enthusiastic about having the parties accept it.

2. See Haynes, "Power Balancing" in *Divorce Mediation, Theory and Practice* (The Guilford Press), 1988, Folberg and Milne, editors, p. 277 and following. Thanks to Ken Cloke for much of this material.

3. A lawyer is not free just to walk away when his client fires him under stress. He is ethically bound to act in the client's best interests, even though, at the time, he no longer may speak for the client. This can be very tricky, as it was here.

4. The power of attention is greatly underestimated in our culture. In negotiations, real listening (open, nonjudgmental) actually changes the nature of the interactions so that discussions may become fruitful. The same is true in the realm of health and healing. Physician Deepak Chopra writes: "When you pay attention to

something, you shift from passive to active awareness. Attention exerts far more control than people ordinarily realize. That is because we are victims of passive awareness. A person in pain is aware of the pain but not that he can make it increase, diminish, appear or disappear. Yet all this is true. People can walk on fire, for example, because they can control their level of pain; more remarkably, they can control whether their feet actually get burned—that, too, is under the control of attention." *Quantum Healing,* Bantam Books, 1989, p. 237.

5. Lynn Sandra Kahn retells the story in *Peacemaking, a Systems Approach to Conflict Management* (University Press), 1988, pp. 137-144, "Case Study #27: Camp David, September 1978." Begin and Sadat are prototypical protagonists in matters of personal style. Yet despite this, a most difficult framework for peace was negotiated over a thirteen-day period through the skill and tenacity of President Jimmy Carter and his team.

6. For a fascinating discussion of power in negotiating, see Roger Fisher, "Negotiating Power: Getting and Using Influence," *American Behavioral Scientist* 27:2, p. 149.

7. See "Three Approaches to Resolving Disputes, Interests, Rights and Power," Ury, Brett and Goldberg, *Getting Disputes Resolved,* 1988, pp. 3-19.

8. Woodrow Wilson said, "Power consists in one's capacity to link his will with the purpose of others, to lead by reason and a gift of cooperation."

9. William F. Lincoln is a principal in National Center Associates, Tacoma, Wash.

11.
MEDIATING EMPLOYMENT MATTERS

It is well to remember that the entire population of the universe, with one trifling exception, is composed of others.
— John Andrew Holmes

Employment: A Fertile Ground For Disputes

The need for mutuality. In American society, employment is the principal staging area for relationship problems outside the family. Employment is often one of the most important relationships in a person's life. Relationships require mutuality — not necessarily equality, but a commitment to mutual gain and an acceptance of each party's "right" to be wrong once in a while.

Without mutuality, it's just a matter of time until something goes seriously wrong. It happens at times that the apparently weaker party, the single employee, becomes the manipulator of the employer, rather than the other way around. While traditionally, it is the employee's needs that aren't met, at times, the employer is virtually powerless to have its needs met.

The tendency to escalate. The employment relationship in the U.S. is heavily legislated and heavily lawyered. This makes problems harder to resolve. There is a tendency to name the action of another in terms of some legal right or responsibility. "Discrimination" might be the label for rudeness, "sexual harassment," for inappropriate behavior and "management right," for a basic lack of consideration. This is not to say there is not *real* discrimination and violation of rights in the work place. The issue is how and when problems get resolved. Early, low level resolutions that satisfy concerns are far better than lawsuits over the failure to resolve those concerns. Most employees, given the chance, would rather not suffer the hurt needed to establish a viable legal claim.

In today's charged employment environment, employees more easily perceive violations of statutory protections. They may see a lack of responsiveness in internal procedures as discriminatory. On the employer side, employee relations professionals (personnel or human resources staff) may quickly label complaints according to legal theory (handicap discrimination, sexual harassment, for example) to comply with accounting mandates from company and government. This has an escalating effect. Lawyers for both employees and employers create entangling webs of strictures on their clients, trying to assure the benefit of some legal remedy, in case it is needed.[1] These are only a few of the forces pulling towards escalation rather than de-escalation of the problem.

Escalation causes the loss of many opportunities to resolve matters at a low level. Those involved become defensive and reactive. Defense attracts offense; a lawsuit is filed and from then on, communication stops. What could be resolved in a day or two by a quality discussion in a safe environment takes on a life of its own, consuming time, money, energy and attention, while returning only grief. For every all-star victory there are hundreds of defeats, boasting no winners.

Employment lawsuits are long, drawn out affairs. One or both parties are likely to rely on the observations and testimony of the employee's co-workers, and the testimony of supervisors and managers will inevitably be involved. By the time the matter might be tried, key witnesses have moved away or disappeared. The depositions, document productions and trial may create or exacerbate problems between co-workers, between employees and their supervisors, or between various levels of supervision and management. Resolution of the case may be achieved only at substantial cost to those involved, as well as to the productivity of the work force and to the profitability of the enterprise. Unjust discharge cases in California were reported in 1988 to routinely cost the employer from $81,000 to $208,000 in attorneys' fees per case.[2]

The lawsuit often obscures the important questions to ask: where are we going, why and at what cost? When can we expect resolution and what can be accomplished? Our thinking is dominated by the wrongdoing of the other side which translates into an unwillingness to talk until all other options have been exhausted.

Disgruntled former employees have done everything from buying a share of stock and disrupting shareholders' meetings, to shooting up the place. Legal remedies often fall short of meeting the parties' needs: back pay may be small or inordinately large, due, perhaps, to the hazards of the job market and delay in reaching trial; a plaintiff may not want reinstatement, and compensatory damages for pain and suffering are available only in certain actions.[3] Punitive damages to teach the offending employer a lesson may be very hard to get. Claims for compensatory or punitive damages as well as RICO (Racketeer Influenced and Corrupt Organization Act of 1970, a popular claim in many actions filed today) may cause the employer to defend as if death itself were the alternative.

Enter Mediation

Mediation is a low level, low impact method of airing concerns too touchy for conventional in-house treatment. It provides a safe place for venting emotions, while the calm discussions that predominate actually get somewhere. It is safe to broach difficult topics, without fear that things will blow up. With a skilled mediator, highly charged situations move from accusatorial to problem-solving.

Offering mediation to an employee implies respect. The vast majority of employees respond with like respect for the employer's integrity and willingness to problem-solve. Employers, too, are beginning to respond favorably to offers to mediate coming from employees, at least where they are represented by counsel or the union.

Mediation works to facilitate a discussion when discharge was merely contemplated, but as yet no action has been taken. An employment relationship that isn't working for the employer usually isn't working for the employee. Both are unhappy. Before things become too adversarial, it is still possible to have a reasoned discussion where each side can evaluate what steps make sense, under the circumstances.

Mediation has been used:

- to initiate discussions over an employee's claim to patent rights;
- to sort out trade secret issues, after an employee has voluntarily left;
- to resolve inter- and intra-departmental frictions;
- to reduce peer group frictions within a department and within an office — including among law firm partners.

Mediation also has been used to improve the quality of contract negotiations, helping to assure that people's expectations match. Its most common use in this field is to transform employment litigation into a mutually acceptable post-employment relationship, through at times, even continued employment or reinstatement are agreed on.

Settlement rates in employment mediations are just as high for pre-litigation situations as for disputes on the eve of trial. Mediating early thus means substantial savings, since in most cases, a lot of lawyering proves unnecessary.

Employers often authorize preliminary legal activities that can cost tens of thousands of dollars. This is called "erring on the side of caution," and cost-justification is not considered. It is, of course, necessary for the employer to do a thorough investigation, headed by someone independent of those with a motive to cover up. It is not necessary that lawyers do this. In fact, using someone focused on building a defense may be counter-productive, for it may block understanding of the larger picture.

Some people equate softness with weakness. In mediation, it is easier to be soft on the people and tough on the problem. This avoids many of the hassles lawsuits engender: parties or counsel snarling at each other, making work of the simplest tasks.

Consider this common situation, often a prelude to a lawsuit.

Innuendoes to Sexual Harassment: A Study in Escalation

Margot has been working for a company we shall call Symmetrex for some five years. She recently requested and received a transfer into the key secretarial post in a new department. She has no problem with the work. It's just the people. Some young engineers hired in the department have her running around bringing them coffee and whenever she walks past one of them, there are audible appreciative sounds. Her boss loves his engineers and is unaware of what is going on. He thinks of Margot as a kid, although she is 26. He is a busy man and to her seems never to have time to listen to any problems she might bring him.

What might happen next?

- **Margot complains to her boss.**

Unlikely. She feels the deck is loaded against her and the subject is not easy to talk about. Nor is he inviting talk from her.

- **Margot complains to personnel.**

Maybe, if they have a unique reputation for protecting confidentiality. Margot isn't one to rock the boat. She doesn't want to become a victim, but she's increasingly unhappy.

- **Margot doesn't complain.**

Likely. The situation becomes an accident waiting to happen, since it is causing her serious distress. It's just a matter of time until the situation festers into something bigger.

· **Margot complains to her fiance.**

Likely. What she does may well be heavily influenced by family and friends. She has nowhere else to turn, as she sees it.

· **One of the engineers goes too far.**

Likely. The situation is unstable in a downward direction.

· **Margot complains to an agency or a lawyer.**

A lawsuit or complaint is filed and served on the employer. Maybe, if someone she knows has had a decent experience there recently. Still, that's more rocking of the boat. She's going to reach this point when she feels the situation is so out of hand, the company needs a lesson, so others won't have to suffer in the way she is suffering. This generalizing is almost always present when a legitimate sexual harassment claim surfaces.

The Reactions of Those Involved

Boss. Surprised. Embarrassed. Angry he hasn't heard about it earlier from her. Blame is often the first reaction.

Margot. Defensive. Furious. Why didn't her boss notice? It was so obvious. Now she's a victim. She didn't want that. Rage is, surprisingly, a form of progress.

Engineers. Surprised. Caught off-balance. Defensive. Angry at Margot for "leading them on." Some are still in denial.

Human Resources. Missed this one. A new label on a new file. How far will this go? No case presents a bigger double bind to an employer.

Management. Critical of lower management and personnel: "Not observant enough, not performing supervisory responsibilities adequately." Seeking counsel advice, investigating. Justifying its position by its carefully choreographed response. The focus is on damage control and preparing the defense.

Legal offense and defense obscure the need for problem-solving. Lit-think dominates: just about everyone is blaming, defensive and self-justifying. The stage is set for months to years of litigation, before anyone mentions the possibility of negotiating a resolution. Early mediation can stop the escalation in its tracks in the vast majority of cases. But who will propose it? Consider the situation from both side's viewpoints.

How Do The Parties Respond?

The employee's dilemma. Lawyers for employees often counsel their clients through the steps of internal complaint procedures. Often they do so with a view to helping secure a resolution without formal proceedings. Sometimes it is also to build a record. With confidential counseling, the employee may gain the confidence to carry the matter forward inside, knowing there is someone in her corner. It also keeps the matter at a low level. Lawyers who represent employees know that the mere appearance of a lawyer for the employee escalates the situation.

With the client's consent, the lawyer may contact company counsel directly. This requires a great deal of trust and confidence; the company can readily build a fence around the employee, in the name of containing the problem. It can become just a matter of time until the employee leaves, often under adverse circumstances. Without a formal complaint or a clear understanding with employer counsel, the employee may be defenseless.

More and more frequently, employees are offering to mediate. This may or may not be done through counsel. Offering mediation has the effect of disclosing the employee's lawyer, who may have been in the background. Many counsel prefer to get some impact from making their presence known. This can be done by attaching to the offer to mediate a proposed charge or complaint. The implied threat simply needs to be evaluated.

Handling the initial rejection. Companies in the past have tended to respond that there is nothing to mediate, not understanding that mediation is simply a tool for productive discussions. If an offer to mediate is rejected, discuss how long it should take before a discussion might be productive. The strategy here is to keep the other party talking about *when* it will be useful to talk. In this way, we change the focus from whether to *when*, a major step forward. Eventually, the employer may see that there is no time like the present. When the weeks and months go by it becomes obvious that if a quality discussion were to take place, a lot more could be done, with less hassle, to everyone's benefit.

The employers' dilemma. Given many companies' hesitancy to use mediation, one might ask, "What is the risk?" Is it the risk that you did something (suggested mediation) when, perhaps, you might have not had to do anything? Is it the risk that by offering to talk in a neutral setting, you are admitting something or perhaps showing weakness?

Employers use early mediation to obtain new information and a fresh perspective. They may use it to telegraph a firm resolve to resist unreasonable demands as well as to make a just settlement. Employees and their counsel almost never see an offer to mediate as a sign of weakness. They may use the mediation forum to impress on the employer their intention to go forward, if no agreement is reached. In the confidential environment of the mediation, these strategies can have considerable impact, but posturing tends to fall away under the intense light of mediation.

If you were the company, what would you want counsel sought out by your employees to do? Could you encourage early, direct contact by counsel for employees? How? The personal relationships that would enable counsel in smaller communities to let your lawyer know they are involved in a matter rarely exist in a large urban environment. And so the matter festers until a complaint is filed. Yet most management lawyers and human resources professionals would probably prefer to do something about every situation in order to catch the one which otherwise will become a blockbuster, perhaps two million dollars in legal fees and two-plus years in litigation — a true no-win. Early contact serves this strategy.

In some cases such as Symmetrex, the company never has a chance to offer mediation, as it only "learns" of the situation after it becomes public. The harassment label is applied and the adversarial process launched. One or more alternative dispute resolution (ADR) resources might have headed this off.

For example, a company could have a program to provide a mediation process at the employee's request. This puts the option forward formally, but not confrontationally. One of the hardest things for employees to understand is the responsibility the company has to provide due process to an accused employee in sexual harassment cases. To the complaining employees, it feels like they aren't being believed. In mediation, the employee can gain some understanding of the employer's situation and vice versa and may help to devise an approach that resolves this difficult situation.

Mediation may also allow employers to act more decisively. In one sexual harassment mediation, the company was so convinced of the wrongdoing of one long-term employee that it terminated him immediately following the first day of mediation, despite the very real risk of having that decision set aside later by a labor arbitrator. It did so to demonstrate solidarity with several very credible women — employees and former employees — and to emphasize its commitment to a decent work environment. Prior to the mediation, it was not willing to take that risk, even though it knew the facts.

An ombuds[4] can help. If the company had an ombuds practitioner, a confidential resource and skilled mediator, outside of line authority and outside of human resources responsibilities, Margot might have consulted with that person and been willing to tackle the problem before any complaint was filed. The ombuds's sole responsibility is to help the employee get the problem resolved, something that more and more companies are finding to be in their self-interest. Human resources can never cover this base fully because by definition these professionals have responsibility for management for the operation of the internal system.

That conflict looms large in employees' eyes when the situation is perceived as particularly sensitive — such as harassment or problems within management levels.

ADR resources within the system help employees deal with just such situations. To provide a work place for people is to take them with all of their human frailties. The question is not whether there will be problems, but whether we can help them to be self-correcting.

Conclusion

Pursuing or defending a lawsuit becomes a consuming passion. The issue changes from what is good for us to what is good for the country. The courthouse is a place for this, but here's the catch: even cases fought primarily for principle rarely go to trial. And there is a terrible economic and emotional price for keeping the grievance fresh for all the years it takes to get to trial.

The best protection against serving as cannon fodder for the great American litigating game is to keep looking for opportunities to talk, to mediate. As Winston Churchill said, "To jaw, jaw is always better than to war, war."

Notes to Chapter 11

1. A beautiful vignette showing how legal advice causes people to overcome their best instincts, with predictable regret, is found in "Rosen, Hers," *New York Times,* Nov. 25, 1982, p. 16, col. 1. This little story is about a bully's mother who failed, on the advice of counsel, to ask after the much younger, hurt child's condition and her later chance meeting of that child's father on a suburban train. It is reprinted in a comprehensive and very thoughtful law school textbook on mediation and other litigation alternatives. If this is what is being taught in law schools these days, things aren't all bad. See Leonard L. Riskin and James E. Westbrook, *Dispute Resolution and Lawyers* (cited above, Chap. 8, n. 2), at p. 202.

2. RAND Corporation's Institute for Civil Justice report, Daily Lab.

Rep. (BNA) No. 182, at A-10 (Sept. 20, 1988).

3. Age discrimination has long been one of the most favored recovery categories in the discrimination spectrum.

4. Mary Rowe, Special Assistant to the President at Massachusetts Institute of Technology and pioneer in the corporate ombuds movement reports that there is some reluctance in many quarters to use the term "ombuds," although it is used. "Ombudsman" was the original term, used in Scandinavia where ombudsmanry originated. "Ombudswoman" is occasionally used. "Ombudsperson" is much more common. "Ombuds practitioner" is widely used in print, though not as a title. What is needed, perhaps, is another Eleanor Holmes Norton who in one fell swoop transformed "chairman" into the far less common term "chair" by designating herself "Chair" of the EEOC when she took that position. Now many people can't remember using any other term.

12. TURBO-CHARGING CONTRACT NEGOTIATIONS

There is nothing more likely to start disagreement among people or countries than an agreement.
— E.B. White, from *"My Day"* in *One Man's Meat*

Have you ever wondered about mediating contract negotiations? Labor negotiations are mediated all the time, but they are often more confrontational than other business negotiations. In negotiations between businesses, communication seems so easy at first. Everyone's getting along. We think, "Why raise sticky issues?" We're trusting that once we build a good relationship, we'll be able to tackle the more difficult points. And after all, there is always the chance we might miss the deal entirely if difficult issues are raised too early.

Perhaps we're the ones seemingly in the driver's seat in the negotiation. The other side will go along with what we want, even if it sounds oppressive, because we have the economic power. Why use mediation?

Mediation As a Tool

The biggest reason for using mediation is that it becomes safe to raise difficult issues. We therefore can take on very sensitive subjects like, "What will we do in the event one of us feels the contract has been breached?" We can also motivate key people on both sides not only to put their all into performance of the agreement, but to address problems early, before communication breaks down.

American contract negotiations often take a long time. Drafts are prepared, then mailed or faxed back and forth. Phone tag begins; other work intervenes. In mediation, the mediator manages the relationship while the parties work, with a word-processor if need be, on revisions which can be reviewed almost as quickly as they are proposed, providing great savings of time.

The most common problem in business relationships is frustrated expectations. When one party thinks it is buying a product and the other thinks it is selling a professional performance such as a construction job or legal services, there's bound to be trouble. The frustrations surface gradually and unless addressed at the beginning, can cause monumental problems down the road. It requires exceptional communication skills, opportunity and a workable structure to handle these as they arise.

The power of mediation may be seen through the following examples of contract disputes which turned into negotiations.

Case example: contract redrawn. One mediation involved a dispute arising out of an agreement to license and develop software for the operation of an Arizona insurer. The parties had reached agreement in rough form on the first day of mediation, through the efforts of their CEOs, the technical teams and counsel. On the second day, they attempted to hammer out a Memorandum of Agreement. That proved extremely difficult, due to personality problems between counsel. One lawyer dotted every "i" and crossed every "t." The other lawyer was a great generalist.[1] As a result, gaining agreement on anything was very difficult. The CEOs and lawyers came to the third day of mediation six weeks later with drafts of settlement documents on which they were hopelessly polarized.

The mediator brought to the third and final day a mediation-trained lawyer who specialized in negotiating such agreements. This lawyer was able to provide the parties with the comfort of knowing how these types of agreements tend to work out in the geographic area where the dispute occurred. At one point, the feuding lawyers even allowed him to meet privately with their clients and the mediator, in order to resolve one particular problem. His contribution enabled counsel for both sides to provide the cautionary advice their clients needed to hear without making agreement impossible. At the end, after ten hours, the parties signed in final eighty pages of agreements which had been word-processed as the mediation went along.

The agreement resolved two arbitrations over a five million dollar computer software development and licensing agreement. Trust had built to the point that the parties agreed to go forward with a modification of the original contract, which had gone astray due to incongruent expectations. The parties were willing to give each other another chance.

Case example: keeping the job going. A school construction project was in trouble. The engineering firm, a subcontractor to the architect, had failed to submit some key calculations and seemed to be dragging its feet. In just a few days, work on the project would be so far behind, the project would stop and penalties would become applicable. But try as he might, the architect's principal could not get the work out of the engineering firm. A mediation, set up that very week, revealed the problem.

The engineering firm had made a fixed-price bid on the basis of some inadequate paperwork, thanks to a partner no longer with the firm. At the time of bidding, it had no idea the scope of work expected of it, and the language in the contract left a big hole. Small wonder its bid was low. It was so unreasonably low, the engineering firm's partner could not imagine the architects didn't know. "Mutual mistake" yelled the engineer, primed as he was by his lawyer for this mediation. "A binding agreement," responded the architect, equally well-advised.

The mediation was convened at the suggestion of the carrier for both firms. Both sides could reach their lawyers if need be, but lawyers weren't present. After an extended joint session, in which the mediator gathered the facts and identified the sticking points, the parties caucused. Typically, the first caucus is to gather additional information the parties might want to keep confidential. In this case, the mediator learned that it was almost impossible for the engineering firm to do the needed work, due to staffing problems. It was apparent that getting the project going was essential to the architect: clearly, there wasn't time to litigate the matter. In subsequent caucuses, the mediator worked with the engineer to figure out how to get the job accomplished and with the architect to better understand how to get the result he needed.

After several hours, the principals reconvened in joint session to work out the details. The architect had an intern with a background in mathematics it agreed to loan the engineer for the weekend and the principal engineer agreed to head the project work himself. It was planned to get the work done and back to the architect by Monday morning, in time to head off stopping the job. An economic settlement was worked out, with variations depending on whether the work got done correctly and on time.

This was a case where neither side could benefit from insisting on its rights. The only possible way to help either side was to help both sides. The convening carrier was motivated, obviously, by a desire not to have two insureds fighting each other. But the quick response of the mediator was also important: every day of delay took options away from the parties. Had the matter been litigated, the damages would have been enormous and all possibility of mutual benefit would have been lost.

Case example: claimed negligence in dam. Two lawsuits over the quality of engineering work on a hydroelectric dam in the Southeast were settled by an agreement that the engineering firm buy out the owner/developer. This mediation began with a draft agreement prepared by a lawyer both sides respected. The problem was, negotiations had broken down.

Participating in the mediation were the local manager and a ranking officer in the company which owned the dam, and the principals of the construction firm with their insurance carrier.

The counsel who had drafted the original agreement was available by telephone.

The mediation lasted thirteen hours. At the conclusion, the parties started to leave, saying "the mediator understands the agreement." "Not so fast," the mediator rejoined. She then had all parties put on tape their understanding of what had been negotiated paragraph by paragraph using the original draft agreement, together with new provisions agreed to in mediation. This tape was transcribed under the mediator's oversight and transmitted to the counsel on whom both parties agreed.

As it happened, the parties agreed on the language of one provision, but for different reasons. When that paragraph came up in the work to get a final agreement drafted, they asked the mediator for her recollection. Each had already accused the other of backing out of the agreement or trying to change the deal. The transcript showed clearly there had never been agreement on the *meaning* of the words in question. The mediator informed them that they both were in error in this respect and they simply needed to negotiate this point now. They did and the settlement held.

Other contract negotiation mediations. There are many other examples of the mediation of complex contract negotiations. The accomplishments of these mediations tell the tale:

- Extended litigation over a patent was resolved by the allegedly infringing company becoming a marketing arm of the patent-holder.
- A marital property dispute was resolved by a viable partnership arrangement for the operation of jointly owned commercial property.
- A silicon chip research and development contract dispute was resolved by negotiation of a new contract.

The Transformative Power of Mediation

In several of these examples, the parties went from being adversaries in litigation to becoming business partners! There is little that can better demonstrate the transformative power of mediation. These transformations could not have happened if each party had not been willing to strive to understand the other side's situation. When they did, they saw the other's point of view as well as the justification for their actions sufficiently to trust them with another agreement.

In business negotiations there are often rough spots. One side might say, perhaps, "Why don't we include a provision for resolving disputes?" The other side might counter quickly, "Why? What do you think might happen to this agreement?" The edginess in the voice might betray a new doubt about the wisdom of making the deal at all: "What do they know that I don't know," one negotiator might be thinking. "What could go wrong here? Have I missed something?" In the honeymoon days of deal-making, who wants to take such a chance?

This tendency to be agreeable, to make no waves, is also evident when business people come together after trouble has cropped up. Lower officials or juniors may have met before, and been unable to resolve differences, perhaps because of decisions by higher management. Eventually, senior officials from each side will come together. They exchange pleasantries, perhaps have lunch or dinner. But there's a real reluctance to tackle difficult or sensitive subjects.

The reluctance is understandable. Each side knows that the next step is likely to be a lawsuit. Often, there is high tension around the topic of concern. What do they do if the thing blows up in their faces? It could be years before there might be another chance to talk. This way, at least the door is still open.

The presence of the mediator changes all of this. A good mediator is patient and tenacious in allaying the anger that can disrupt discussions. An example is the mediation of a $30 million construction dispute that had been in litigation for a year and a half. In the mediation, a key executive on one side was so angry about what he saw as the other side's negligence that at times he could hardly speak. Finally, on the morning of the third day of this mediation, he looked up suddenly after the other side had completed an explanation on one point and said, "Oh, yes. I see what you mean." The tension in the room melted visibly. The mediator and others took a deep breath. It was time to begin. The negotiations eventually bore fruit in several major agreements.

Conclusion

When things grow tense, the mediator redirects people's attention. Perhaps there's a comment or story that allows people to laugh, or the mediator will talk about how this type of problem has been handled in other mediations. The mediator may simply call a break and give people a chance to stretch. Quick, informal caucusing with each side can elicit enough information to allow the mediator to change the focus so more information can be developed, or to give the issue a rest. There is an infinite number of strategies; good mediators learn to pick appropriate ones for each situation.

Perhaps the best explanation for the powerful interface between contract negotiations and mediation is this: negotiation is an art form. It reaches its highest form with highly skilled, sensitive negotiators and a supportive environment. When a skilled mediator provides that environment, understands the negotiation game and knows how to support the parties at every turn, the negotiation has a lot more going for it. It is a small investment with big returns.

Notes to Chapter 12

1. The two were the American lawyer versions of Menacham Begin and Anwar Sadat. See n. 5, Chapter 10.

13.
CHARTING PUBLIC AND PRIVATE POLICY

Impasse is in the eye of the beholder.

The World We Have Made

Are you happy about the condition of the world? Do you feel your local, state and federal governments — employees and officials — are doing what they should be doing? How does politics strike you? Can you see someone like yourself getting involved in politics? When you hear on the news how in so many disputes, one side is screaming at the other side, do you feel that progress is being made? Or do you find yourself suspicious of leaders' motives and of both governmental action and inaction?[1]

This is the world we have made. American values supporting individuality and *rights* have left the equally strong historical American values of cooperation and collaboration in the dust. In my lifetime, "collaboration" came close to being synonymous with treason, as the oppression of Cold War thinking made fear a way of life in the 1950s.

There is a feeling of helplessness that sometimes comes from listening to the news. But there is reason for hope. Below the reach of the spotlights and sound-bites we are reclaiming our heritage of trust, here in America and around the world. Little by little, we are letting go of the fear of each other that has dominated human society for millennia. Problem-solving, sometimes called collaborative problem-solving, is calling us to a new day.

Beyond disputing. Courts, agencies and private organizations are finding that it is more productive to let people discuss problems in a protected environment such as mediation than merely to satisfy the obligation to hear each side out with an adversarial proceeding. In the adversarial proceeding, there is no exchange of ideas, no reasoning with demands. These can only take place through discussions.

But how does one make such discussions productive?[2] One approach is through mediators and facilitators. Another is the consensus process.[3] Facilitators are often assigned a variety of pre-negotiation tasks. These include working with the conveners[4] — those who are inviting others to participate — to learn who has an interest or stake in the situation. An analysis of these stakeholders might include what they want to achieve and what incentives might get them to join in a discussion.

In addition to a stakeholder analysis, the facilitator might help devise a proposed set of ground rules for the group to consider adopting. Facilitators also help to develop an agenda that will make it easier for the group to reach consensus. Sometimes, facilitators provide logistical support for the discussion group, such as arranging the time and place of meeting, and taking and distributing minutes. For those of us brought up on instant gratification, this may seem laborious and time consuming. But as the computer generation reminds us, garbage in, garbage out. The quality of the discussion depends on laying a firm foundation. And the more people invest in the process, the more they get out of it.

Mediators and facilitators may provide the additional service of conducting the meetings. Mediators are more pro-active than facilitators and must develop sufficient trust to work privately with participants. Some experts recommend using a mediator whenever caucuses or confidential meetings between group sessions are necessary. Mediators may even propose mutually advantageous agreements when the participants run out of ideas, which facilitators generally would not do.[5]

Mediators in public policy disputes do concern themselves

with issues of overall fairness and the workability of agreements. It is considered legitimate for them to focus attention on the attributes of a good outcome but not legitimate to steer the negotiations toward a particular outcome. As with all mediation, the agreement, if any, must be that of the participants.

The parties or participants in a public policy discussion also need to prepare themselves. Their preparation would include determining several things:

- *What are the main issues that need to be negotiated?*
  It is no simple task to frame the issues such that, when they are resolved, all participants' concerns are met.

- *What are the secondary issues within each issue that need to be negotiated?*
  There may be sub-issues within the primary issue that need to be identified.

- *What side agreements (not among all parties) might be needed in order to make overall negotiated agreement among all stakeholders more likely?*
  In a mediation to set priorities for a long-term statewide environmental program, for example, you might need a side agreement between a company and the enforcement agency, allowing a manufacturing facility a fixed amount of time to clean up its site on its own.

- *Are there procedural agreements which need to be reached, in order to keep the group discussion progressing?*
  Take, for example, a mediation over proposed regulation of public land grazing. Ranchers and the government might agree to postpone changes in their leases, pending the outcome of monitored tests of new approaches to grazing management, that offer the opportunity to restore the damaged land.[6]

- *What procedural agreements need to be reached first?*

> For example, in the mediation of a lawsuit over Indian fishing rights, it might be imperative to start with a joint fact-finding process, to narrow the areas of disagreement.[7]

All of these questions lead you to the drafting of an agenda. Imagine devising that agenda so that as members of the group work through it, they are led to reach an agreement everyone can subscribe to. It is obvious that this preparation work requires a lot of attention and a fair amount of skill. But the payoff is enormous: those parts of your agenda and your priorities that survive in the crucible of a joint process may become the agenda and priorities of your group, your community and even your nation.[8]

Further steps in preparation for a public or quasi-public dialogue include the following:

- *What set of ground rules for the discussion would help participants to jell as a group and be able to accomplish its goals?*
  This would be submitted to the group for approval or amendment. Examples of such rules might be that every member must attend every meeting, that participants speak for themselves, not for their groups, that criticism be reserved for appropriate times and be constructive, or that no press comment be made except by a designated representative.

- *Who should facilitate or mediate the discussion?*
  The individual needs to *be* neutral and also to *be seen* as neutral. He or she also needs to be capable of understanding the issues under discussion.[9] Sometimes insiders, government or private officials, are used as neutrals, if they are not perceived as having a political stake in the outcome of the discussions. Otherwise, outsiders are preferred.

The level of detail involved in simply preparing for a public policy dialogue speaks volumes about the nature of the process. The exercise of going through these preparation steps, as well as those required to make the meeting itself productive and to follow up on progress in the group meetings, invests parties in arriving at an agreement all can subscribe to. It is the opposite of an adversarial process.

Building Community

Mediation and facilitation are now being used by Americans at all levels of society. An example is found in rural Oregon. By 1991, the Oregon Economic Development Department (OEDD), was convinced that top-down efforts to help communities face catastrophic losses in the timber industry were futile. Only efforts "owned" by the communities could make a difference and that meant a "from-the-ground-up" model.

In 1992, Rural Development Initiatives, Inc. (RDI), a non-profit organization founded by Lynn Youngbar with financial assistance from OEDD, began operating.[10] Its facilitators are invited in by community groups or officials. After a preliminary SWOT assessment (strengths, weaknesses, opportunities, threats), RDI staff then guide a series of meetings. These take members of the group through the steps of identifying what they like and don't like about the present situation and what they would like to see happen in the future, which becomes a vision statement. This forms the framework for establishing medium-term goals affecting business and workforce development, infrastructure and quality of life to achieve the vision. From the vision, the group may develop a prioritized action plan to accomplish these goals. RDI provides information about what other communities are doing and access to other resources such as mediation, where needed.

In many communities, leadership is deterred by unwritten rules which discourage speaking up. RDI's facilitators help free people to become productive citizens again. RDI provides leadership training for some community members who have participated in the planning process and supports a network of such leaders across the vast expanse of rural Oregon. It also provides assistance in projects revitalizing downtown areas, converting old mill sites and addressing product development issues in the tourism industry. Through these efforts, it is showing communities how to reverse the nationwide trend toward the decline and death of rural communities.

Through facilitation and by use of mediation as needed, communities are often turning around economic, population and resource decline and beginning the move back to health. In the past two years, more than two dozen communities have established and are implementing plans to guide their destiny. Ten more are in the beginning stages. Private funding now matches public funding in supporting this catalytic work.

Burns is a small community in the wide open southeastern part of Oregon. It is where my mother was born. When the lumber mill shut down for two years in 1979, the town's heart stopped. The mill reopened with 300 jobs and things began looking up. When it finally closed in 1989, Harney County lost 1,500 of its 8,500 residents. Unemployment soared to twenty percent. Stores on Main Street closed; vacancy signs sprouted like flowers on the sagebrush in late summer. Many predicted ruin. But a tough-minded gathering of citizens from all walks of life formed a group to talk about their mutual problems. This was a first. They called in RDI and brought in a consultant to assess the community's strengths, weaknesses, opportunities and threats. From there, they began a planning process.

Things started turning around. The power of people with a common goal, a vision of what might be, working together is phenomenal.[11] *Real discussions* take place. People stop making speeches and begin to hear what others are saying. More important, they become committed to the process, because they own it. And they begin to see that only when everyone owns it, do things start to happen. Today, every store on Main Street is occupied and there is a new Payless store. The weekly seven a.m. meetings of everyone who cares to come are on track and lively.

On sensitive issues such as water, logging, grazing, and mineral extraction, mediation is often required in these communities. In this context, mediation, too, helps people find how to live together in peace and prosperity, to recognize and discard destructive patterns of interaction and to learn from experience that they, personally, can make a difference.[12]

Conclusion

The problems that face people all over the world are very similar and are becoming most compelling. But human nature is a resource as well as a liability. Mark Smith, Executive Director of the Burns Chamber of Commerce, says, "It's attitude. We started working on our attitude, with beautification projects, for example. We just changed our attitude." It might help to think of mediation and consensus as attitude-adjustment tools.

What people world-wide want out of life is much the same. As we approach the millennium, are we willing to commit our own fortunes to collaborative processes such as consensus and mediation? Can we afford not to do so?

Notes to Chapter 13

1. "In the United States," write Lawrence Susskind and Jeffery Cruikshank, "we are at an impasse. Public officials are unable to take action, even when everyone agrees that something needs to be done.

   Every effort by public agencies to shift priorities in response to new problems is met by fierce resistance from organizations that are content with the status quo. Media campaigns, intensive lobbying, referendums, and similar strategies give these groups substantial leverage.

   The courts find it difficult to impose their will. Groups unhappy with court decisions press their legislators to change the relevant laws. Cases come back again and again on appeal as single-minded groups seek to have things their way." *Breaking the Impasse,* (cited above, n. 3, Chapter 4), p. 3.

2. There are many reasons why unassisted negotiations fail, among them that the issues are too many or too complex; the full range of stakeholders was not obvious; and all key parties were unwilling to engage in joint fact finding and perhaps the alternative to negotiation looked acceptable. Susskind and Cruikshank, *Breaking the Impasse,* (cited above, n. 3, Chapter 4), p. 239.

3. The goal of the *consensus process* is a decision that is consented to by all group members. It does not mean that everyone must be completely satisfied with the final outcome. Rather, the decision must be acceptable enough that all will agree to support the group choosing it. Although it is an ancient process, it has been used extensively by the Religious Society of Friends (Quakers) for over 300 years.

   It is a slippery concept for many people brought up on majority rule, but its promise is powerful. When everyone *really will* support a group decision, little can stop it. All those fights down the road that follow the decision-making traditional in our society are avoided, *provided* the participation is broad enough. The members' commitment to the process, which is also needed, may grow during the group process.

   The durability and strength of decisions reached by consensus is the answer to criticisms that it takes too long. This commitment need not be present at the outset, but may grow during the group meetings. See *A Handbook for Consensus Decision-Making, Building United Judgment,* Center for Conflict Resolution, 1981.

4. Lack of confidence in the process and clarity in the goals on the part of its initiators can not only be fatal to its success, but also add to the cynicism that may defeat subsequent collaborative efforts. See, "Mediating Conflict Over Dioxin Risks of Resource Recycling: Lessons from a Flawed Process," Nash and Susskind, *Environmental Impact Assessment Review,* 1987, vol. 7, pp. 79-83.

5. See n. 1, Susskind and Cruikshank, p. 140 and following.

6. Allan Savory, author, wildlife biologist and consultant, has sparked a movement to restore holistic management practices to the land. He argues that with the loss of vast herds of wild animals, we must use livestock to restore the land to fruitfulness. He celebrates the interrelationship of all life, from micro-organisms to predators, and is teaching ranchers and government officials how to use animals to heal the land. His approach centers on creation of a common goal, much as consensus and mediation do. Rejecting purely economic approaches, he teaches how to improve the quality of life, reduce debt and live again in harmony with the land.

Savory, *Holistic Resource Management,* Island Press, 1988.

7. This checklist is adapted from a 1992 Teaching Note developed by Scott T. McCreary and John K Gamman of CONCUR, a nationwide environmental and public policy training and mediation firm with offices in Berkeley and Santa Cruz, California.

8. A guide for citizen action is offered by Susskind and Cruikshank, p. 204 and following. See n. 1.

9. See n. 6.

10. Conversation with Lynn Youngbar, founder and president of Rural Development Initiatives, Inc., (RDI) January 14, 1994.

11. Stephen R. Covey calls it synergy, a super-charged, exciting adventure in creativity. *The 7 Habits of Highly Effective People,* Simon & Schuster, 1989, p. 262 and following.

12. For example, the Confederated Tribes of the Umatilla Indian Reservation secured mediation over a $100 million Columbia River water management project. Involving state and federal agencies, Water Watch of Oregon, Oregon Trout and the Oregon Natural Resources Council, several irrigation districts and the Tribes, this matter was mediated in five full-day sessions over a period of less than three months by a professional mediator and a water law expert. As a result, tribal fishing rights, made meaningless through depletion of the streams, were to be resuscitated, with irrigators becoming members of a team working to replenish the salmon runs. The cost to the parties was roughly $20,000. The mediation was reported in *Consensus,* Harvard Project on Negotiation, July, 1992, p. 1.

14.
STRATEGIES FOR PEACEMAKING

The essence of being human
is that one does not seek perfection.
— George Orwell, from "Shooting an Elephant,"
in *Reflections on Ghandi.*

A peaceful system is one tending toward stability while allowing for change. It is dynamic, not static and it requires constant attention.[1] Tipping the balance toward peace and away from violence, war and other adversarial activities requires "concrete and localized acts of peace."[2]

There are three fundamental strategies for making peace on a day-to-day basis. Following them will help align values, goals and the means for achieving them — within organizations and within individuals.

Keep Talking

Whether or not you understand the other side of the situation, keep the dialogue going. Talk around the point, if necessary, not always to the point. As an old teacher of mine liked to say, there is more to talking than flapping your gums. Even in the biggest shouting match, some of the words going across the table carry useful information. In the heat of the fray, stop. Listen carefully to what you are saying and what the other side is saying and not saying. Isn't there something there on which to build a discussion?

The willingness to listen, to keep discussion going, is effective even if it only comes from one side. Patience is the touchstone. In one mediation, the parties were at loggerheads. A charitable organization was in the process of remodeling an old hotel in a Midwestern city to create a retirement facility. Its board of directors was squared off against two design firms, demanding damages for delays. The architects were demanding fees. The negotiation consisted of the board repeatedly forwarding its demand for delay damages. Each time, the architects explained how the contract and the situation at the job site showed that the problem was the absence of a competent contractor.

Once again, the board would lay out its demand. In the course of the four-hour confrontation, the architects had kept talking, not just about why the delay damages claim made no sense, but about a variety of issues, throwing in such information as the situation permitted. The tension was enormous.

Eventually, the board caucused to reexamine its priorities. The board's real concern, upon reflection, was to get the facility built within the loan commitment. As this became the focus of discussions, differences began to narrow. After fourteen hours, an agreement was struck which made a great deal of sense to each side: both fee claim and damage claim were dropped.

The local architect agreed to stay on the project to help the board get someone competent on the job site to run the job. This successful resolution could have been lost if the architects had been impatient with the seeming stalemate earlier in the mediation. It might never have been found if the board had not paused to examine its priorities.

This is not to suggest that steps needed to prepare for trial should not be taken. For example, in some states, special masters have been much used to facilitate discovery in complex cases and also to promote settlement.

The coercive nature of mandatory use of such masters means that parties may not feel comfortable in trying to extricate themselves from a settlement process long after its usefulness to the parties has vanished.[3] If the talks are not productive after a time, it makes sense to go forward with trial preparation, perhaps checking in through mediated discussions at strategic points along the way.

Speak From the Heart

Speaking from the heart means speaking honestly. It does not require compulsive truth-telling. It means refraining from expressing something different from what you feel, whether the expression is verbal or in non-verbal communications — a shrug, a smile, a frown, for example.

Children's remarkable ability to ask penetrating questions no one else seems able to ask derives from the fact that children's words, thoughts and feelings are aligned. If they don't understand, they haven't yet learned to say they do. They never heard of a "stupid" question and don't put up a front. Many people believe it is sophisticated to say what they think people want to hear. It is true you cannot be a good negotiator if your feelings are on your sleeve. But really good negotiators are authentic, honest, fully congruous in feelings and words or actions. This congruity gives them an authenticity which engenders trust. It does not make one an open book. It makes one trustworthy. Expert negotiators act in ways consistent with credibility.

Consider an employee who has just been told to do something he doesn't believe is right. A response of, "Oh sure, no problem," deprives his boss of the opportunity to check the proposed action herself to see if it really is what she wants done. It deprives both of the chance to see if there might be a better way to do what is needed to be done. And it creates an untruth between them, which is likely to cause trouble later. Yet the honest expression of the employee's reservations will not occur unless trust between the two is at a sufficiently high level.

If we are committed to speaking congruently, we respond better after the fact when some excess we've committed is brought to our attention. We recognize and acknowledge the overkill and let it go. The knee-jerk defense or explanation, auto-speak — talk generated out of reach of the heart — is much more common. But it has no place in an environment of authenticity.

Be Respectful of Others

Respect is the greatest tool for peace-making. To show respect, we find ways of trying to put ourselves in the other's position. This is not the same as being "nice." It is far deeper, far richer. We don't jump on others for not being able to express what they mean perfectly, seizing on their words, disinterested in any subtleties of meaning. Instead, we look behind the words to the feelings. We are open, receptive, interested, attentive, tough on the problem, but gentle on the people.

Johnny Moses, a Northwest Indian shaman, teaches about the pointing finger: "Whatever you accuse another of, is three times more true of you." Look at the other three fingers of your hand as you point and you'll see where this wisdom may come from. Blaming is still in fashion, but it evaporates into a new understanding of personal responsibility under this teaching. I have seen a group of workshop attendees suddenly deprived of words by it, as the members strove to explain their personal situation in terms of their parents' failings.

Our keenness for another's faults or weaknesses derives from our own unconscious self-judgment, for it is things we disown in ourselves that we most resent in others. The charge, "you're just being manipulative," comes, often, from a manipulator. It is only by loving and respecting our imperfect selves that we can ever respect others.[4]

Conclusion

Litigants in this country spend more than $30 billion a year on lawsuits and the legal system. Imagine what those dollars could do, kept at home. That is only a small part of the reward for peacemaking. The other part of it is the development of a passionate interest in mutual gain, based on a recognition that relationships need to work for all or they work for none.

The Constitution of UNESCO (United Nations Educational, Scientific and Cultural Organization) provides:

> Since wars begin in the minds of men, it is in the minds of men that the defenses of peace must be constructed.

So let it be. For all our sophistication, we Americans are strangely weak in dealing with conflict. Einstein provided an important footnote:

> The significant problems we face cannot be solved at the same level of thinking we were at when we created them . . .

The measure of success in resolving disputes is not how many chickens each side walks away with, but how well-equipped and motivated we are to move beyond disputing, to go on about our business. Only by walking mindfully in the paths of peace in our personal and business lives can we hope to restore peace and harmony to the planet. In this task, mediation excels.

Notes to Chapter 14

1. "Democracy is never a final achievement. It is a call to untiring effort, to continual sacrifice and to the willingness, if necessary to die in its defense." John F. Kennedy

2. See Chapter 3, n. 1, "The Violence Among Us," Bernd Huppauf.

3. See Chapter 5, n. 8, Lee Novich.

4. "Techniques for Getting in Touch with Your Disowned Selves" are presented in the excellent book, *The Tao of Negotiation,* Harper Collins, 1993, at p. 161 and following by Joel Edelman and Beth Crain.

APPENDIX 1
DECOMPRESSION EXERCISE

(This is based on the work of Edith Stauffer, director of Psychosynthesis International, teacher and author of *Unconditional Love and Forgiveness*.)

Breathing has long been a vehicle for increasing self-awareness, something that is hard to achieve in our busy, urban lives. Self-awareness in the context of resolving differences means recognizing our own contribution to the continued difficulty and deciding to do something about that. The body is also a great teacher, as this experience demonstrates.

Set aside a full five minutes. You may want to tape the following material for playing back or have another person read it slowly to you as you do the exercise. With a tape, you can pause it as you do the exercise, when you need more time. Without either of these aids, simply read the material to yourself a couple of times before beginning.

Make yourself comfortable. Close your eyes and breathe slowly and deeply. Allow the breath to fill you deeply. Exhale all of the air, slowly, fully. Notice how relaxed you feel at the end of each breath, in that quiet space before the next breath begins.

Allow intruding thoughts to drift away, without any effort on your part. It is counter-productive to chastise yourself for having these thoughts. You are in a space beyond blame, a place of action and consequences rather than who's right and who's wrong.

Check your face muscles, your jaw, your shoulders, your back for tension. Allow your shoulders to fall back and down, noticing the comfortable stretch. Wiggle your toes. Imagine the breath going to any place in your body that hurts or is tense. As you exhale, imagine that each breath carries with it a little of the pain or tension you are feeling.

Put your hands on your belly and breathe into it for a moment, noticing if there is any feeling of fear or anxiety there. It is said that fear lives in the belly and that it is the child in us who fears. Comfort that child in you that is anxious or afraid by thinking of all the goodness and happiness in your life. Let yourself be like a baby — warm, comfortable, breathing easily.

Now recall the dispute. Notice what happens to your body, as the thought of these difficulties floods your mind. Notice your face and jaw muscles, your back, your belly. Now take the recollection of the dispute and in your imagination, put it on a little shelf just to one side of your head. Clear your mind by breathing deeply and slowly again three times and concentrating on the feeling of your breath passing your nostrils.

Next, remember a time when you felt really good about yourself. Relive that experience in your imagination now, re-experiencing the sounds, sights, smells and feelings it brings back. What a great time of your life! Revel in it, for it is part of you. Notice how relaxed your body feels. Notice your jaw and face muscles in particular. Hold the recollection of that experience, for you will use it as a filter.

Now holding on to that good experience, gently retrieve the recollection of the events of the present dispute. Keep breathing. Keeping in mind the good experience, just let these events replay. Notice if the whole situation seems to have lost some of its power. Keep breathing.

Now stretch, wiggle your toes, open your eyes when you are ready. Look at the situation with new eyes, loving yourself for the good you've done and tried to do, forgiving yourself for the errors. Look at the other person in the same way. When you can fully appreciate their view, including, perhaps, how unattractive what you did or failed to do appears — when you get past the "yes, but," and past your own self-blame — your perspective is in balance.

Done properly, this exercise evokes compassion and moves you beyond judgment. You can now view the situation dispassionately enough to make sound decisions in your own best interest.

Most of the time, people find that the events leading to the dispute are softened and in some way rendered more responsive by this exercise. Sometimes they realize that before doing the exercise, what happened seemed to carry a personal attack. Afterwards, it becomes just another event. Sometimes, even though we know that it is we who are hurting, we're not ready yet to stop. If you find the exercise doesn't help, be patient. Do it again in a few weeks and perhaps in a few months. Imagine thinking about this person, this event, with no stress, with no emotional spin on it at all. That is within your grasp.

APPENDIX 2
WRITING AGREEMENTS IN MEDIATION

Whatever agreements are reached in mediation are wisely captured in written form at the time. More and more counsel bring draft settlement agreements to the mediation. As Louise Lamothe, first woman chair of the American Bar Association's Litigation Section writes:

> It is best to document the agreement on the spot. This often requires some doing, since the session may conclude in the wee hours of the morning (in fact, that seems to be the rule). To handle those problems, I bring a notebook computer loaded with sample settlement agreements. Using the computer, we draft and plug in specific language to implement the settlement. Often this process exposes other issues that the mediator can help the parties to consider, using the goodwill developed during the mediation.

Postponing such documentation to another day has many pitfalls. Most annoyingly, the momentum toward resolution developed during the mediation dissipates when the lawyers return days later to the task of writing the agreement. Sometimes clients (and lawyers) find ways to raise new issues or alter agreements; the process can then falter, often taking weeks to conclude and sometimes unraveling.

It is not unusual to see the counsel working together, one at the keyboard, one or more standing by. Sometimes it is the mediator at the keyboard. Everyone strives for agreeable language; the mediator may also propose language. Redrafts of key paragraphs are done until they are satisfactory.

The process is time-consuming, but moves at light-speed compared to trying to negotiate such agreements by telephone and facsimile, when everyone has turned to other business. In one mediation of a gender-based wrongful termination case, it took sixteen hours to reach agreement and four more to conclude the settlement agreement. The lawyers brushed aside their fatigue as best they could in order to secure closure. The clients were well-served and well-pleased. Although the plaintiff had a week to revoke the agreement, it held.

Working up an agreement in mediation saves weeks to months of delay and significant expense. In addition, in cases with strong emotional currents, it is far easier to get a signature at the time of the mediation than later. Even if there is a statutory revocation period, such as the seven-day waiting period in age discrimination matters, the signature at the time is an important token of intent to reach finality.

Interim agreements. All mediation can lead to interim agreements on procedures which, when followed, will lead to resolution. Various mediators are more or less likely to keep the parties focused long enough to get to this stage if overall agreement proves impossible at the time. It is your responsibility to request this discussion whenever you feel it appropriate.

If the mediation is early, its most productive use may be to win agreements on procedures for collecting and disseminating information everyone now sees is needed. You may have taken a run at settling a case that seemed too small to justify much pre-mediation effort. You may have a big case which cries for a highly effective working relationship among counsel. Mediation develops this.

If it appears that adjudication will be necessary, the parties may readily negotiate an agreement on issues to be presented for decision, stipulations to be reached and what scope the parties will have in presenting evidence or arguments. For example, one can negotiate a pretrial order or an agreement for binding arbitration. This can save the parties an immense amount of time, effort and expense.

Final agreements. Negotiating the terms of a final agreement can be time-consuming. It is helpful not only to have a draft settlement agreement in hand, but to have considered which paragraphs will need negotiation and to have some options in mind with respect to these. For example, if confidentiality of the settlement terms is required, what difficulties might be encountered in negotiating for this? What alternatives might you consider?

Or again, if future action is to be required by the agreement, who is motivated to do it? Who will take care of the details? How will you know when it is done? What agreement might you seek to assure needed compliance? Do you want to negotiate any fall-back arrangement, if it isn't done or is not done in a timely manner?

Dispute resolution clause. Always include a dispute resolution clause in the agreement. At the minimum, this should provide for mediation. If your mediator has been satisfactory, name her as mediator for any dispute relating to performance or interpretation of the agreement.

In long-term construction contracts, joint administrative committees are sometimes constituted, primarily to head off problems of differing interpretation. Sometimes, a mediator is provided for, should this group be unable to reach agreement. Differing expectations are often the biggest headaches in contract administration. It is best to recognize and deal with these early, before frayed tempers make productive discussions impossible. Particularly in the construction arena, time is of the essence. Yesterday's options are slipping away; today's options will be gone in a few more days.

APPENDIX 3

METHODS OF DIVIDING PROPERTY

(Ken Cloke, Center for Dispute Resolution, Santa Monica, Calif.)

The following are techniques used by lawyers and mediators to help parties reach agreement over the division of property.

Mutual Selection:

Each party places their initials next to the items they want, then they discuss contested items in terms of who selected it or uses it, and attempt to reach agreement.

Barter:

Each party takes certain items of property in exchange for other items. For instance, the car and furniture in exchange for the truck and tools.

One divides, the other chooses:

One divides the property into two parts and the other gets to choose between the parts. Or one chooses first and the other second, rotating until all items are divided.

One values, the other chooses:

One places a value based on present fair market value on each item of property and the other gets to choose items totaling one-half the total value.

Appraisal and alternate selection:

A third person such as an agreed upon appraiser places a value on contested items of property, then the parties choose alternately.

Sale:

Some or all of the items are sold and the proceeds divided equally.

Secret bid:

Each party places a secret bid on each contested item of property and the one who bids highest for the item gets it. Where one party receives items that exceed their share, there will be an equalization payment to the other party.

Private auction:

The parties openly bid against each other on each item of community property. If one receives more than his or her share, an equalization payment will be made.

Mediation:

The parties negotiate, using a mediator.

Arbitration:

The parties select an arbitrator who will make the final decision about valuation and division after hearing from both parties and considering all the evidence.

APPENDIX 4
THE EMOTIONAL STAGES OF DIVORCE

Introduction. Particularly visible in divorce situations are the emotional aspects of conflict. The emotional stages of divorce are the same as those found in any situation where one or another side feels wronged. There is the *denial* ("This can't be happening to me"), the *rage* ("He, she, they can't do this to me") and eventually the *acceptance* ("It happened to me, I had a part in it, I've been hurt, but the remedy is sufficient under the circumstances"). This material is included to make this process more visible.

Denial. As with death, the first stage in reacting to divorce is denial. Mediators work with the parties to get them to accept the fact of their separation, and *choose* it or a return to marriage counseling to discover whether the marriage is in fact over. Divorce brings one or both parties the end of a consistent source of self-definition. Denial is triggered when a party has no sense that a better, happier self-definition may emerge from separation.

Anger. Following denial comes anger. Mediation allows divorcing parties to experience the full range of emotions appropriate to their separation. It then becomes possible to change incrementally, to evolve from one stage to another without compromising the process or detracting from its result. The expression of anger at the opposing party may help both move on to agreement. In mediation, power remains with the participants rather than with the mediator. Attachment to objects, so troublesome in legal proceedings, in mediation leads to better understanding of the emotional tides of divorce. For example, mediation allows a couple to use the children or the money or Aunt Mary's chest of drawers to act out their sense of abandonment, entitlement and acceptance of loss. The object in dispute is allowed to become "irrelevant" (metaphorical) or "practical" (problem-solving). Once the anger is dissipated, mediation then lets them choose solutions based not on anger, but on present needs.

Acceptance. Agreement and acceptance grow out of the progressive refinement of individual needs in the negotiation. They do not depend on objective abstract criteria as in law or subjective or internal processes as in therapy. At a certain point it becomes obvious that anger is not working and, when a person is ready, a choice can be made to give the anger up, since anger is a way of maintaining a negative kind of intimacy. The surrender of anger is the first real acceptance of the fact of divorce.

There are important differences in the emotional states each party experiences during their separation. Mediation acknowledges, respects, annotates and comments on their progression through these states. The parties' interim working compromises chronicle their resolution.

Reconciliation can be achieved in mediation — not necessarily in the sense of a return to marriage, but of creating a friendship out of intimate knowledge of the other, a common history, and a lack of compulsory attachment. For many divorcing couples the rage is too recent to consider reconciliation. Yet the glimmerings of future friendship are often evident at the conclusion of the mediation. This parallels the pattern of processing business disputes as well, for human nature is a constant.

APPENDIX 5
FAMILY MEDIATION: TWO CASE STUDIES

The first story involves a relationship that had become a shell, yet an unstated threat of suicide hung over any effort to make the breach official. The second is the story of how two parents deepened their love for their son, as they struggled to reach agreement on custody and visitation issues. In each, there are lessons which directly translate into the world of business mediation.

Case Example: The Husband Who Lost Interest in Life

Jim and Frances were married in Chicago in 1953, then moved to Los Angeles, where they bought a home and raised three children. Frances worked as a secretary and Jim worked as an aerospace engineer.

Jim was a quiet, proud man, uncomfortable with emotional communication. His first response to confrontation was a kind of sullen withdrawal, which angered Frances and made her more shrew-like and bitter.

Their silences grew deeper, their separations longer. Jim eventually withdrew into the garage not only to work, but to sleep, watch TV, and drink. Thirteen years went by as the chasm between them widened and the silence grew deafening.

When their youngest began college, Frances declared the marriage over and asked for a divorce. Jim was angry and uncooperative, as he had been for years. Frances's lawyer recommended mediation. Jim at first refused, but Frances persisted, threatening a court battle if Jim would not participate.

First mediation session. Sensing Jim's resistance, the mediator turned to Frances. She said there was a big discrepancy between what Jim preached and what he practiced, that she no longer trusted him, that he was an alcoholic who had been arrested twice for driving under the influence. "That was three or four years ago," Jim grumbled.

Jim said that he, too, was unhappy in the marriage. It became apparent that for Jim to move out and separate successfully from Frances, he needed to overcome his fear of suicide or death as a consequence of his ouster from the garage. He had no hobbies, no special interests; he didn't go away on vacations and said he didn't enjoy much of anything. Jim was 59.

The mediator became more active. Since Jim and Frances were separating, he did not have to stay at home. Of all the places in the world where he could go this year, which would be his favorite? He answered clearly and with the first glimmer of positive feeling. Oregon! The mediator got Jim to expand on this — showing him a way out of resistance and fear.

The mediator spoke openly now about the fear of separation and death. Jim described the pleasures of self-discovery and creation of a new life for oneself on one's own terms, replete with visions of time spent woodworking in Oregon. Frances listened in amazement and began to hope that he would find something that would make him happy.

The mediator then shifted the discussion to issues that needed to be resolved. The first of these for Frances was that Jim find another place and move out. Jim again became resistant and did not understand why he had to move out so soon.

Frances was asked to tell him why. She said with great bitterness and anger, "Because you're driving me crazy. I want to get on with my life and I can't with you holding me back. I want to reorganize the house, and I want you and your things out." Jim at last understood.

Jim said he would begin looking for a place, but had no idea where he would go. The mediators asked many questions designed to make Jim's move real to both parties. Would he speak to real estate agents or look in the newspapers? Would he rent or buy? Did he want to be close to work or his kids? How long did he need to look and when did he plan to move out?

When the discussion was turned to property, Frances said she wanted to keep the house, and Jim agreed reluctantly. Later he stated that his interest was in holding onto his retirement policy, which was worth a considerable sum. They both were given homework assignments to get accurate figures for all the assets and asked to return for another session.

Second mediation session. At the second meeting a few weeks later, Jim had still not moved out or located any place to live, and Frances was furious. The mediator acknowledged her feelings, noting that the longer it took to separate, the more their anger at each other would grow, causing their relationship, poor as it was, to worsen.

The mediator then asked Jim what efforts he had made to find a new home. Jim had been looking, he said, but found nothing that was suitable. The mediator supported these efforts and asked what he planned to do next. Jim finally agreed to set a deadline for moving out.

The mediator went on to discuss the division of assets and support, putting definite numbers in place of rough guesswork, and making tentative allocations to one or the other. Again, they were given homework, to list all the possible solutions and get final figures for several items. In the interim they were sent a list of possible solutions developed by the mediator.

Third mediation session. When they returned after the deadline, Jim still had not moved out, and Frances was even angrier. Again the mediator encouraged Frances to express her anger and acknowledged her frustration and rage. Jim, recognizing that violence was becoming a possibility, agreed to move out that weekend without fail. Frances accepted this and later Jim made good on his promise.

The positive aspects of the divorce were beginning to emerge.

The mediator encouraged Jim and Frances to visualize what their lives would be like if they could lead them exactly as they wished. They were encouraged to compare their visions with their life before, in a marriage lived apart, with only the door into the garage in common. They observed that the door not only closed them off from each other, but from their own true selves. They realized their divorce began 15 years ago. Now they had an opportunity to complete it and to make it positive by each creating for themselves their own lives as they wanted them to be.

Final figures were gathered and put in place and a plan was developed in which Frances got the house and Jim got the retirement plan. Each had some cash available and Jim would pay off the mortgage. The alimony would be paid by a money market account which would accumulate with company contributions for the next three years while Jim continued on payroll. Both received just what they wanted.

Frances and Jim thanked the mediator and said they felt the result was fairer than they thought possible. Everyone shook hands and departed. The mediators later learned that Jim had indeed kept his word about moving out.

The lawyers' role. In this mediation, the lawyers provided the mediator, confidentially, with critical information their clients needed to have included in the agreement. At their suggestion, the mediator, an experienced family lawyer before becoming a mediator, drafted the initial agreement which was critiqued by the lawyers as the mediation progressed. The final version of the agreement had both counsel's approval.

Case Example: Shared Custody

Sara had been blind from birth. She had also been the victim of sexual abuse. While she had gone on to become a competitive athlete in the special Olympics, she had not established a successful sexual relationship.

She dated Bill for about six months in 1978, but they never married or lived together, as she said she did not want a sexual relationship. According to Sara, Bill had raped her. Bill denied this. Sara, however, became pregnant. She said nothing to Bill and had the baby alone.

Two years later while in counseling over the after-effects of the alleged rape, Sara decided to confront Bill with his child. At first Bill denied it. How could she know it was his? It took some time for him to realize that Scott was his son, and he had many misgivings about what had happened.

Bill began to see Scott for a couple of hours on Saturdays, gradually increasing their time together over the years. He began to pay child support, and agreed that it was not enough. The situation worsened dramatically when Sara and her mother came to suspect that Scott had been molested by Bill's mother. Although they later withdrew the charges, believing them unfounded, Scott was taken from Sara's home and from his father, and eventually sent to Sara's sisters, who refused to let Bill see him.

Sara and her mother hired an attorney, and while Bill felt he had been supportive of them, he discovered in court that he was not represented or recognized as Scott's father. All the latent hostility between Sara and Bill came out in court and the child abuse case became a custody dispute. Bill hired an attorney on his own and secured a joint custody order with visitation every other week. The hostility and suspicion continued.

Sara now had a relationship with Ted. They decided to move to a small town about four hours from Los Angeles where she and Bill had lived and worked and Scott, now 7, had gone to school. She gave short notice of her decision to move to Bill and none to the court.

Bill applied for and received a temporary restraining order against her removing Scott from Los Angeles. Based on his allegation that Sara was in violation of the court's prior order regarding joint custody and visitation, he was also awarded sole custody, with week on/week off physical custody.

School was set to start in one week, both sides were at complete loggerheads, and trial was set for October. Both sides had spent tens of thousands of dollars on legal fees and were no closer to a solution. In desperation, Sara's attorney decided to try mediation. At first Bill was reluctant to come to mediation and refused to pay for it. Sara was unable to pay. The mediators agreed to begin the mediation without an agreement to pay their fees, and told the couple that if they felt at the conclusion that it had not been helpful, they would not be asked to pay for the session. Mediators know the value of the process and at times are willing to work in this fashion.

A male-female attorney-therapist team began the mediation, as each party seemed interested in having someone present they could confide in. When asked to give an opening statement, Sara deferred to Bill, but as he spoke, she continued to interrupt him. Bill threatened to leave if she continued, which became difficult because she was unable, due to blindness, to take notes for later reference.

Initial staging. As a tactic, the mediators shifted back to Sara, but her details were less informative standing alone than when delivered in response to Bill's narrative. She disliked the custody schedule. She said the transitions were difficult and it was hard for both her and Scott. Sara said that when Scott returned from Bill's it was constant videos and non-stop talk about ninjas, Superman and other escapes into fantasy.

At the mediator's insistence, Sara said she wanted to see Bill and Scott become close. She did not want to interfere in that relationship. At the mediators' request, she repeated this to Bill, only more directly and emotionally.

Bill told her how much he loved his son and said he was willing to do whatever was necessary to help him. He loved Sara also, and told her so directly, but recognized that they were unable to get along. He had extended her a standing invitation to talk, but she always hung up the phone or walked out.

He agreed the every-other-week schedule was not perfect. He had moved a few months earlier to an apartment only a block from Sara's house so Scott could walk over. He appreciated Sara's acknowledgment of his relationship with Scott and felt joint custody was a compromise he could agree to for Scott. He said he wanted to see Scott all the time but recognized that he needed his mother also. He felt Sara should have given him more notice and consulted with him rather than just announcing her move. As real communication began to take place, the subject of the alleged rape was never mentioned.

Options development. The mediators thanked the parties and summarized their principal points, noting that both parents wanted what was best for their son and recognized his need to spend as much time as possible with each of them. They pointed out how much harder it was for Bill and Sara to agree on what had happened in the past than what would work best in the future.

The mediators then briefed the parents on the operational context for their discussions, noting that many parents who live far apart exchange their children during school holidays; that many psychologists counsel against switching children too frequently from school to school; that children generally prefer not to switch schools just before graduation; that courts often prefer mothers as primary custodial parents for younger children, and fathers for older children and adolescent boys; and that as Scott grew older he might want to have a say in where he would live during the school year.

The parties then created an agenda for the negotiation, including where Scott would spend his school year, where he would spend his holidays, travel arrangements, communication, and child support. Each parent wanted to have Scott. The mediators asked whether they would consider dividing the elementary school grades into two sets, 3rd and 4th grades, and 5th and 6th.

Bill indicated he was willing to work things out and to be more generous than he had planned before beginning the mediation. He offered to have Scott live with Sara for two years, then with him for two years, spending school holidays and every other weekend with the non-custodial parent. Sara agreed.

Agreement. The mediators began to write down the principal points of agreement, which included drop-off times and places, an agreement to be flexible but to make these exchanges a priority, an agreement to take Scott's wishes into consideration for junior high and high school, to meet again over communication problems and child support, and to return to mediation if there were any problems. Bill suggested they see Scott together after the mediation and tell him together what they had decided. Sara agreed.

Acknowledgment. The mediators congratulated both sides on their willingness to compromise. It was obvious to everyone that Scott was lucky to have two parents who loved him so much. They noted how difficult it was for Bill and Sara to continue to acknowledge and respect one another. The mediators suggested some rules for continued communication and for keeping Scott's interests in the forefront of their discussions. Bill paid for the mediation, and as he and Sara left, reached over and hugged her. She reciprocated.

While both parties and their attorneys thought there was no chance for a mediated solution before the process began, a single session produced agreement on major items. This is not uncommon. The only risk of trying mediation is the minimal amount of time and money invested, and the willingness to listen to the other side.

Conclusion

Family mediation works because it acknowledges and values human needs and interests and does not rely on memory or credibility. It

- is collaborative rather than confrontational;
- lets quiet people speak and talkative people be quiet;
- surfaces hidden agendas;
- permits dialogue to take place in the language of metaphor;
- encourages the parties to tell the subjective and emotional truth;
- allows for constructive feedback without the appearance of judgment;

allows both sides to see the problem as a whole.

It also allows parties to "fine-tune" a result or change their minds and empowers both sides to say no. Issues break down into "bite-sized" bits and become easier to resolve. Creative remedies may be invoked. The synergy between the parties is used to bring about agreement.

The most important benefit from a societal point of view, perhaps, is that when mediation is well-done, the parties substitute internal for external constraints and thus avoid enforcement problems. This is consistent with the results of the victim-perpetrator mediations, discussed in Chapter 7, where restitution is made by offenders to victims of crime far more often than without the benefit of a mediation process.

Bibliography

A Handbook for Consensus Decision Making, Building United Judgment, Center for Conflict Resolution, 1981.

Administrative Office of the U.S. Courts, *Report of the Director,* Twelve Month Period Ended June 30, 1989 - Appendix 1, Detailed Statistical Tables 36, 1989, n. 14 at p. 134.

Alschuler, "Mediation With a Mugger: The Shortage of Adjudicative Services and the Need for a Two Tier Trial System in Civil Cases," 99 *Harvard Law Review*, 1986, pp. 1808, 1822.

American Arbitration Association, 46 Arbitration Journal 3 (Sept. 1991).

American Bar Association, Model Rules of Professional Conduct, Rule 1.2 and 1.2(a).

Avruch and Black, "Ideas of Human Nature in Contemporary Conflict Resolution Theory," *Negotiation Journal*, July, 1990, pp. 221, 225, 227.

Baruch-Bush, Robert A., "Mixed Messages in the *Interim Guidelines*," *Negotiation Journal*, 9:4, October, 1993, pp. 341-347.

Brill, Steven "Headnotes: The New Leverage," *The American Lawyer*, July/August 1993, pp. 65, 66.

Burkhardt, Donald A., and Conover, II, Frederic K., "The Ethical Duty to Consider Alternatives to Litigation," *The Colorado Lawyer*, February, 1990.

Burkhardt and Conover, II, "The Ethical Duty to Consider Alternatives to Litigation," *The Colorado Lawyer*, February, 1990, pp. 249-251.

Burns, Robert P., "The Appropriateness of Mediation: A Case Study and Reflection on Fuller and Fiss," 4 *Journal on Dispute Resolution*, 1988, p. 129.

Burton, John W., *Resolving Deep-rooted Conflict: A Handbook*, 1987.

California Judicial Council, *Justice in the Balance, Report of the Commission on the Future of the California Courts*, February, 1994.

Charter of UNESCO.

Chopra, Deepak *Quantum Healing*, Bantam Books, 1989, p. 237.

Church, Jr., T., Carlson, A., Lee, J., & Tan, T., *Justice Delayed: The Pace of Litigation in Urban Trial Courts* 1978.

Cochran, Jr., Robert F., "Legal Representation and the Next Steps Toward Client Control: Attorney Malpractice for Failure to Allow the Client to Control Negotiation and Pursue Alternatives to Litigation," 47 *Washington and Lee Law Review* 819, 823-24, 1990.

Consensus, Harvard Project on Negotiation, July, 1992, p. 1.

Covey, Stephen R., *The 7 Habits of Highly Effective People,* Simon & Schuster, 1989, pp. 262 and following.

Edelman and Crain, *The Tao of Negotiation,* Harper Collins, 1993, pp. 70-72.

Ehrlich and Ornstein, *New World, New Mind*, Simon and Schuster, 1989.

Fisher and Ury, *Getting to Yes,* Houghton, Mifflin Co., 1981.

Fisher, Roger, "Negotiating Power: Getting and Using Influence,"*American Behavioral Scientist* 27:2, p. 149.

Fiss, "Against Settlement," 93 *Yale Law Journal* pp. 1073-90, 1984.

Forester, John, "Planning in the Face of Conflict: Mediated Negotiation Strategies in Practice," Chapter 6 in *Planning in the Face of Power*, 1990, pp. 82-106.

Freedman, Haile, Bookstaff, *Confidentiality in Mediation: A Practitioner's Guide*, ABA Young Lawyers Section, 1985.

Friedman, George H., and Silberman, Allan D., "A Useful Tool for Evaluating Potential Mediators," *Negotiation Journal*, 9:4, October, 1993, pp. 313-315.

Fuller, Lon, *Mediation — Its Forms and Functions*, 44 S. Cal. L. Rev. pp. 305, 307-309, 318, 324, 327-330, 1971.

Gary Gwilliam, Gary, former president, California Trial Lawyers Association. Conversation of March 16, 1994.

Gimbutas, *The Lauguage of the Goddess*, Harper and Row, 1989, Introduction.

Green, Eric, "A Heretical View of the Mediation Privilege," 2 *Ohio State Journal of Dispute Resolution*, p. 1, 1986.

Grillo, Trina, *The Mediation Alternative: Process Dangers for Women*, Yale Law Journal, 100:1545, 1991.

Haig, Julie, Executive Director, San Diego Bar Association, Conversation of October 27, 1993.

Haynes, "Power Balancing" in *Divorce Mediation, Theory and Practice*, 1988, Folberg and Milne, editors, The Guilford Press, page 277 and following.

Henry and Lieberman, *The Manager's Guide to Resolving Legal Disputes: Better Results without Litigation*, 1985.

Honeyman, Christopher "Five Elements of Mediation," *Negotiation Journal*, 4:149-158.

Honoroff, B., Matz, D., and O'Connor, D., "Putting Mediation Skills to the Test," *Negotiation Journal* 6:37-46, esp. 37, 40.

Huber, Peter W., *Liability*, Basic Books, Inc., New York, 1988, pp. 3, 4.

Huff, Marilyn, *Fast Track: Reduces Court Delay*, J. Contemp. Legal Issues, pp. 222-227, 1989.

Huppauf, Bernd, "The Violence Among Us," New York Times, Op-Ed, Nov. 21, 1993, p. E 17.

Interim Guidelines on the Selection of Mediators, see Test Design Project.

Kahn, Lynn Sandra, *Peacemaking, a Systems Approach to Conflict Management*, University Press, 1988, pp. 137-144, "Case Study #27: Camp David, September 1978."

Kolb, Deborah M., *The Mediators*, Massachusetts Institute of Technology, 1983. See also her latest book, *When Talk Works*, Jussey-Bass, 1994.

Lambert, Wade, "Calls for Guidelines on Mediation," *Wall Street Journal*, October 22, 1993.

LaMothe, Louise, "Opening Statement: Thinking of Mediation," *Litigation Journal*, 19:4, Summer, 1993.

Lovenheim, Peter, *Mediate, Don't Litigate*, McGraw-Hill Publishing Co., 1989.

Lynn Youngbar, Conversation of January 14, 1994.

Matz, David E., "Some Advice for Mediator Evaluators," *Negotiation Journal*, 9:4, October, 1993, pp. 327-330.

McCreary, Scott T., Gamman, John K., and Tietke, Cornelia, *Using Joint Fact-Finding Techniques to Resolve Complex Environmental Policy Disputes*, CONCUR working paper 92-02, (1992).

Melamed, James, Conversation of February 15, 1994.

Menkel-Meadow, Carrie, "Measuring Both the Art and Science of Mediation," *Negotiation Journal*, 9:4, October, 1993, pp. 321-325.

Menkel-Meadow, "For and Against Settlement: Uses and Abuses of the Mandatory Settlement Conference," 33 *UCLA Law Review*, pp. 485-514, 1985.

Nash and Susskind, "Mediating Conflict Over Dioxin Risks of Resource Recycling: Lessons from a Flawed Process," *Environmental Impact Assessment Review*, 1987, vol. 7, pp. 79-83.

Note, "Protecting Confidentiality in Mediation," 98 *Harvard Law Review*, p. 441, 1984.

Novich, Lee, speech, *What To Do When a Claim Strikes*, the Association of Engineering Firms Practicing in the Geosciences, National Meeting, April 8, 1991.

Ornstein and Ehrlich, *New World, New Mind*, Simon and Schuster, 1990.

Pollock, Ellen Joan, "Victim-Perpetrator Reconciliations Grow in Popularity," *Wall Street Journal*, October 28, 1993.

Potter, R. Clifford, "Your Ethical and Fiduciary Obligations in the Settlement of Disputes," *ALI-ABA Course Materials Journal*, vol.15, n.3, p. 99.

RAND Corporation, "Institute for Civil Justice Report," *Daily Lab. Rep.*, BNA, No. 182, at A-10, Sept. 20, 1988.

Reavley, Hon. Thomas M. "Consider Our Consumers," 14 *Pepperdine Law Review*, 787, 788, 1987.

Reed, Richard C., ed., *Beyond the Billable Hour*, ABA Section of Economics of Law Practice, 1989.

Resnik, "Due Process: A Public Dimension," 39 *University of Florida Law Review*, Spr., 1987.

Ricker, Darlene, The Vanishing Hourly Fee," *American Bar Association Journal*, March, 1994.

Riskin, Leonard L. and Westbrook, James E., *Dispute Resolution and Lawyers*, West Publishing Company, 1987, p. 210.

Riskin, Leonard, "Mediation and Lawyers," 43 *Ohio State Law Journal*, 29, 43-48, 57-59, 1982.

Rogers, Nancy and McEwen, Craig, *Mediation, Law, Policy and Practice*, Clark, Boardman, Callahan, 1989, p. 26, sec. 5.2, p. 47.

Rosenberg, Joshua D., "In Defense of Mediation," 33 *Ariz. L. Rev.* p. 467, 1991.

Ross, Lee, and Stillinger, Constance, "Barriers to Conflict Resolution,"

Negotiation Journal, October, 1991.

Salem, Richard A., "The *Interim Guidelines* Need A Broader Perspective," *Negotiation Journal*, 9:4, October, 1993, pp. 309-312.

Savory, Allan, *Holistic Resource Management*, Island Press, 1988.

Schrader, Charles R. , *Construction Mediation Booms*, Oregon State Bar Bulletin, February/March, 1992, p. 36.

Singer, Linda, *Settling Disputes*, "Mediating Between Farmers and Lenders," Westview Press, 1990, pp. 95-98.

SPIDR Commission on Qualifications, *Report: Qualifying Neutrals: The Basic Principles*, 1989, National Institute for Dispute Resolution (NIDR).

SPIDR Committee on Law and Public Policy, *Report 1, Mandated Participation and Settlement Coercion: Dispute Resolution as it Relates to the Courts*, 1990.

Stillinger, Epelbaum, Keltner & Ross, "The Reactive Devaluation Barrier to Conflict Resolution," *Journal of Personality and Social Psychology*, 1990.

Stauffer, Edith, *Unconditional Love and Forgiveness*, Triangle Phblishers, 1987.

Summers, Robert and Atiyah, Patrick, *Form and Substance in Anglo-American Law*, Clarendon Press, Oxford, 1987.

"Survey of General Counsels and Outside Counsels" by Deloitte & Touche, 1993, reported in *Dispute Resolution Times*, AAA, Fall, 1993, pp. 1-3.

Susskind and Cruikshank, *Breaking the Impasse, Consensual Approaches to Resolving Public Dispute*, Basic Books, 1987, pp. 33.

Test Design Project, *Interim Guidelines for Selecting Mediators*, NIDR, 1993, p. 3.

The Recorder, San Francisco, February, 1994.

Ury, Brett and Goldberg, "Three Approaches to Resolving Disputes, Interests, Rights and Power," *Getting Disputes Resolved,* pp. 3-19, 1988.

Wilkinson, John H., ed., *Donovan Leisure Newton & Irvine ADR Practice Book,* John Wiley & Sons, 1990, Preface.

Wulff, "A Mediation Primer," *Donovan, Leisure, Newton & Irvine ADR Practice Book*, pp. 113-136, John H. Wilkinson, ed., 1990.

"Colorado Adopts Ethics Rule," *Alternatives to the High Cost of Litigation,* May 1992 at pp. 70, 71.

"Ethical Considerations in ADR," *Arbitration Journal*, March, 1990, vol. 45, n.1 at p. 21.

Index

A

B

C

D

E

F

G

H

I

J

K

L

M

N

O

P

Q

R

S

T

U

V

W

X, Y, Z

About the Author

Barbara Ashley Phillips is a professional mediator. She introduced mediation into business disputes in the early 1980s as founder of American Intermediation Service in San Francisco. She mediates a wide spectrum of practical and technical issues, ranging from disasters to lawyer malpractice, from construction to sexual harassment, from aviation accidents to complex contract and environmental issues.

Phillips teaches negotiation and mediation skills and consults on settlement negotiation strategy and design. She has served on the Deep Foundation Construction Industry Roundtable and as ADR consultant to the Aviation Defense Managers Council. She has taught at Golden Gate Law School, University of San Francisco Law School and the University of Santa Clara Law School, in Northern California.

Phillips was born in Oak Park, Illinois, in 1935. She grew up in Portland, Oregon, and attended College of William and Mary. She graduated from the University of California, Berkeley, with a degree in international relations. A graduate of Yale Law School, Phillips practiced law in Oregon City and Medford, Oregon, and in San Francisco, California, where she also served as an Assistant United States Attorney.

She has two sons, Matthew and John, and resides in Halfway, Oregon. She continues to travel to mediations throughout the country.